Hawthorne Revisited

Management and the Worker, its
Critics, and Developments in
Human Relations in Industry

By HENRY A. LANDSBERGER
Professor of Industrial and Labor Relations
Cornell University

New York State School of Industrial and Labor
Relations, *a statutory college of State University of*
New York, Cornell University, Ithaca, New York

Preface

THIS monograph is addressed to both master and student in the field of industrial sociology, specifically, and in the broader field of industrial relations, generally. It has two purposes, one descriptive, the other evaluative.

Our summary of *Management and the Worker* is based on the assumption that in most courses in industrial sociology, human relations, or personnel, it is desirable to introduce the students, whatever their age and experience, to the Hawthorne Studies. Reading the original in its entirety is usually not feasible, while concentration on one part of the book—for example, the Bank Wiring Observation Room—results in ignorance of the greater part of the studies. Chapter II is, therefore, intended as a very sober summary of the entire book, different from many of those extant today in its more complete coverage, in impressing the reader with the great variety of topics and methods touched on and used, and in the realization that every one of the Hawthorne Studies grew out of the inconclusiveness of the one preceding it.

Chapter III is likewise descriptive. It consists of a comprehensive coverage of the criticisms of the human relations school. *Management and the Worker* is rarely attacked separately. It is, however, invariably included in the attacks made on the school to which it is said to belong. Many teachers in this field may wish to have their students acquainted with these criticisms, and we hope they will find it helpful to have an extensive selection brought together in one place and arranged in the logical pattern which they in fact form.

Beginning with Chapter IV, however, this monograph evaluates and explains rather than describes; first, with respect to *Management and the Worker,* then, in Chapter V, more generally with respect to the Mayo school and its development over the last twenty years. The tone of these chapters is deliberately somewhat more protective of the Mayo school than this author generally feels, since it seems time that the balance of criticisms were redressed from their present state of almost complete one-sidedness. We hope to demonstrate that *Management and the Worker* deserves better treatment than has been accorded it, and that the school in general has a far better case than is normally conceded.

The author wishes to thank Mrs. Elaine Adams for an almost magic touch in her editorial work and Mrs. Carol Seidenberg and Mrs. Lucy Straus for their valuable efforts in the same direction; his wife Betty for extensive help on Chapter III; his colleagues Donald Cullen, Frank Miller, and Oscar Ornati for their thoughtful comments; William F. Whyte for his tolerance and encouragement; and Josephine Richards and Katherine Anderson for long-suffering patience in typing and retyping this manuscript.

Grateful acknowledgment is made to the Harvard University Press for permission to quote and, in Chapter II of this monograph, to summarize extensively material from *Management and the Worker.*

H. A. L.

Ithaca, New York
February 1958

Contents

		Page
	Preface	iii
I	Introduction	1
II	The Hawthorne Studies	4
	The Introduction to the Studies	5
	Part I: The Rest Pause Experiments	7
	Part II: The Analysis of Complaints	16
	Part III: Understanding Employee Attitudes	18
	Part IV: Common Environment and Group Formation	21
	Part V: Applications	27
III	Criticisms of the Mayo School	28
	Social Change and Anomie	30
	Image of the Worker	35
	The Function of Collective Bargaining	39
	The Place of Unions	43
	Conclusion	46
IV	The Hawthorne Studies: Guilty as Charged?	48
	The Question of Antiunion Bias	51
	Image of the Worker	55
	Anomie and the Causes of Industrial Conflict	63
	Lessons for Manipulators	73
	Summary	78

CONTENTS

V The Hawthorne Studies and the Development of Human
    Relations in Industry............................ 80

Some Problems in Defining the Human Relations
    Approach..................................... 81

Reception and Timing: The Discovery of Workers'
    Resistance to Change.......................... 86

Problems for Theory in an Applied Field.......... 90

The Corrective Function of a Comprehensive Study:
    Two Examples from *Management and the Worker* 96

The Stimulating Function of a Comprehensive Study:
    The Development of Human Relations—A Cau-
    tionary Tale................................. 100

Developments in Human Relations in Industry—
    Their Roots and Direction..................... 107

Summary and Conclusion........................ 113

Index... 117

There are some books which cannot be adequately reviewed for twenty or thirty years after they come out.
—JOHN MORLEY

→ CHAPTER I ←

Introduction

EVER since the appearance of the Hawthorne Studies in the late 1930's, a war has raged over the writings of what has become known as the Mayo school. The Fort Sumter of this war—and it is a civil war among sociologists at least as much as an interdisciplinary war between sociologists and economists—was Gilson's review of *Management and the Worker* in the *American Journal of Sociology*.[1] Earlier comment, in the *American Sociological Review*, on Whitehead's *Leadership in a Free Society*[2] and *The Industrial Worker*[3] had been only mildly critical. No call to battle, these, although Lynd's review of the latter book in *The Political Science Quarterly*[4] was far from flattering and could also qualify as the opening shot.

The publication in the middle forties, however, of shorter books summarizing these studies and drawing more general conclusions from them was taken as a *casus belli* by a variety of outsiders, from editors of *Fortune* to university professors all over the United States and Western Europe. In fact, a most spectacular academic battle has raged since then

[1]Mary B. Gilson, "Review of *Management and the Worker*," *American Journal of Sociology*, Vol. 46, No. 1, 1940, pp. 98–101.

[2]Fred R. Yoder, "Review of *Leadership in a Free Society*," *American Sociological Review*, Vol. 3, No. 1, 1938, p. 104.

[3]Goetz A. Briefs, "Review of *The Industrial Worker*," *American Sociological Review*, Vol. 5, No. 1, 1940, pp. 146–147.

[4]R. S. Lynd, "Review of *Leadership in a Free Society*," *Political Science Quarterly*, Vol. 52, 1937, pp. 590–592.

—or perhaps it would be more accurate to say that a limited number of gunners has kept up a steady barrage, reusing the same ammunition. The gunners have been joined recently even by some representatives of management who have begun to question the validity of the human relations approach.[5]

The beleagured Mayo garrison, however, has continued its existence behind the solid protection of factory walls. According to one of the senior lieutenants of the garrison,[6] the attackers' heavy pressure has not been without effect. Both union and management problems have now been studied. Training in human relations is being given a critical look by the field itself because of evidence that it is ineffectual,[7] and the influence of environmental, technological, and structural factors on in-plant relationships is being studied. Despite these efforts to accommodate the critics, no immediate cease fire is to be expected. The virtual absence of any direct response from those under attack[8] leaves the attackers smarting under a severe feeling of being slighted, makes peace negotiations impossible, and makes a continuation of the war pleasant since the hazards of a counterattack by the besieged are apparently negligible. In view of this lamentable state of affairs, and the prospect of its indefinite continuation, a plea is being entered here to remove from the field of carnage, and to salvage for a more objective appraisal, the Jenkins' Ear of this Armageddon. The reference is, of course, to *Management and the Worker,* the book upon which most of the controversial summaries and interpretations of the Hawthorne Studies are based.

[5]Malcolm P. McNair, "What Price Human Relations?" *Harvard Business Review,* Vol. 35, No. 2, March–April 1957.

[6]W. F. Whyte, "Human Relations Theory—A Progress Report," *Harvard Business Review,* Vol. 34, No. 5, 1956, pp. 125–132.

[7]Cf. Edwin F. Harris and Edwin Fleischman, "Human Relations and the Stability of Leadership Patterns," *Journal of Applied Psychology,* Vol. 39, No. 1, 1955, pp. 20–25.

[8]Three exceptions are G. C. Homans, "Some Corrections," *Review of Economics and Statistics,* Vol. 31, 1949, pp. 319–321; S. Chase, "Comment," *Antioch Review,* Vol. 10, 1950, pp. 405–406; C. M. Arensberg and G. Tootell, "Plant Sociology: Real Discoveries and New Problems," in *Common Frontiers of the Social Sciences* (Glencoe, Ill.: The Free Press, 1957), 310–337.

This monograph is therefore devoted to a very thorough reassessment of *Management and the Worker,* not only in the light of the criticisms leveled against the book and against the Mayo school generally, but also in the light of its relationship to subsequent developments in the field of human relations in industry. Such a re-evaluation seems particularly appropriate at present because the entire field has recently been subjected to assessments of a more exhaustive and objective kind than heretofore. Argyris at Yale[9] has described the direction taken by research in some of the major subdivisions of the field, while the Industrial Relations Research Association has published a volume which is not only descriptive but also critically evaluative.[10] It seems appropriate to round off these evaluations with an assessment of the work which is unanimously regarded as the pioneering one in the field.

It should be made clear, however, that we are embarking on a genuine evaluation—that is, neither an outright defense nor a total attack. While it will be our ultimate conclusion that the book is a classic which still has many lessons to teach us, we shall criticize it on some major points in reaching this conclusion. The reader expecting a black-or-white approach will be disappointed and may sometimes wonder how it is possible to praise here and criticize elsewhere. This, however, is what we believe the book merits. Further, our defense will as frequently take the form of saving the book from its friends, and what they have read into it, as of defending it from its enemies. In particular, we shall make some distinctions between *Management and the Worker* and the writings of Elton Mayo, and show that the data and their evaluation by the authors is often as close to that of Mayo's critics as it is to Mayo's own approach. We say this despite the fact that Mayo had over-all responsibility for the studies and based his later thinking on his interpretation of them.

[9]Chris Argyris, *The Present State of Research in Human Relations in Industry (A Working Paper),* Yale Labor & Management Center, 1954.
[10]Conrad M. Arensberg et al., *Research in Industrial Human Relations: A Critical Appraisal* (New York: Harper & Brothers, 1957).

3

CHAPTER II

The Hawthorne Studies

In *Management and the Worker* are reported a series of social psychological and industrial psychological studies which were carried out at the Hawthorne (Chicago) plant of the Western Electric Company between 1927 and 1932. The research reported in the book was a cooperative venture between the company (which is engaged in the manufacture of telephone equipment) and various units of Harvard University, of which the Graduate School of Business Administration was the most prominent. Before the publication of this volume some of those who participated in one or another of the studies had already published their own reports (for example, North Whitehead's *The Industrial Worker*). But *Management and the Worker,* which appeared in 1939, some seven years after the conclusion of the studies, was and remains the most comprehensive account of the investigations as a whole. Although written by only one member of the Harvard team, F. J. Roethlisberger, and one representative of the company, W. J. Dickson,[1] many more persons participated in the planning and conduct of the so-called "experiments."

The book is a formidable one, containing more than 600 pages, 34 tables, and 48 figures. Perhaps because of this, many readers have ignored it in favor of condensations which they

---

[1] The title page acknowledges also the assistance and collaboration of Harold A. Wright, chief of Personnel Research and Training Division at the Hawthorne Works. But the book is generally referred to as the work of the two senior authors.

have had no particular reason to question. The "illusion of familiarity" with the experiments, to which Mayo referred in his preface to the book, was by no means wholly dispelled by the book's publication (p. x). It is for this reason that we have thought it worth while to describe in some detail the sequence of experiments contained in the book. We shall not only describe the findings at each stage but give special emphasis to the steps which led from one experiment to the next.[2] We consider this emphasis quite an appropriate one in view of the book's avowed purpose: to present "the course...and continuous history of the entire series of experiments" (p. x), and the authors' admission: "In most cases the results obtained, instead of giving definite answers to the original questions, demanded a restatement of them" (p. 3). In short, a new research step was taken by the authors most frequently because of the admitted inconclusiveness of the previous findings. "A constant shift to inquiries not anticipated in the original plan became characteristic" (p. xii).

The Introduction to the Studies

The book opens with a statement that the various studies covered by it would be dealt with in sequence, and that the authors would not only present the results of each study, but also the "trials and tribulations" encountered en route. In the first chapter, the authors give a brief resumé of the formal organizational structure of Hawthorne; a description of the personnel policies in force at the plant in the mid-twenties (the company was noted for its extensive welfare program); and a brief description of the three so-called "illumination experiments."

These experiments, although sometimes thought of as part of the Hawthorne Studies, were actually conducted in advance of the bulk of the studies included in the book, for they were

[2]Two other comprehensive summaries are to be found in Milton L. Blum, *Industrial Psychology and its Social Foundations* (New York: Harper & Brothers, 1956); and Delbert C. Miller and William H. Form, *Industrial Sociology: An Introduction to the Sociology of Work Relations* (New York: Harper & Brothers, 1951).

undertaken between 1924 and 1927, before the studies which formed the body of the book had even been planned. They were conducted in collaboration, not with Harvard University, but with the National Research Council, and the authors include them only because their results provided the stimulus for later studies.

The experiments were conducted in three series. In the first series, three departments—each engaged in a different kind of work—were studied. In all three departments, illumination was progressively increased. But despite this similarity in experimental treatment, production did not react in the same way. In one of the departments, production fluctuated randomly relative to illumination; in the other two departments, production did increase with the increase in illumination but erratically so, seemingly independent of the increase in illumination.

Since some of these differences in effect might have been due to differences in the type of work performed by each department, and also to differences in the types of workers employed in each department, the second series of illumination experiments was conducted in one department only. Two groups of operators were chosen so as to be comparable in terms of age and experience. One of these groups—the control group—continued to work under the conditions of illumination to which it had been accustomed. The other group—the test group—worked under varying lighting intensities. The results were once again perplexing since the production of both groups increased to an appreciable, and identical, degree.

Those directing the experiments thought that the unforeseen results of the two previous series of experiments might have been due to the combination of artificial with natural illumination which had been used. Therefore, a third series of studies was conducted, essentially repeating the experimental design of the second series, but employing only artificial light at decreasing intensities. For the third time, results so far as production was concerned were different from what had been expected; production in both the control and the test group rose steadily. Only when the illumination for the test group became extremely low did production suddenly fall off. Further, minor experiments showed that the intensity of light under which operators thought they were working was at least partly independent of the actual intensity, since operators in two instances thought the illumination under which they were working was being increased and decreased, respectively, when in fact it remained steady.

The results of these experiments indicated not only that experimental groups who worked with progressively greater illumination produced more (which was fully expected), but that groups produced more who did not have more illumination, and indeed, even those groups whose illumination was progressively decreased, produced more. Whatever the relation between illumination and productivity, it could not be disentangled from the influence of other variables. No detailed interpretation of these seemingly contradictory results was, therefore, attempted. The scientific value of the studies was seen as no greater than that of serving as "a great stimulus for more research in the field of human relations" (p. 18). Essentially, the authors' puzzlement over the results of the illumination experiments was the taking-off point for, and the link with, the Relay Assembly Test Room experiment, in which the effects of variations in another kind of working condition—rest pauses and length of working day— were to be investigated. The description of the planning of this latter experiment marks the proper beginning of the book.

Part I: The Rest Pause Experiments

The authors' purpose in conducting the Relay Assembly Test Room series of experiments was to investigate further the determinants of an individual's productive efforts (this first part of the book is titled "Working Conditions and Employee Efficiency"). This time, however, they wished to do so under conditions which would allow them to eliminate, or at least to control, the variables which in their opinion had confused the outcome of the illumination studies. For example, in order to facilitate more accurate measurement of productivity itself, employees were selected for study who were producing a part (relay assemblies), the output of which was determined chiefly by the employee rather than by any machinery which might be "pacing" him or her. Moreover, these assemblies were sufficiently standardized and were produced often enough to enable productivity, and even slight changes in productivity, to be easily measurable. But it should be noted that the emphasis was still on the study of physical— not of psychological—determinants of productivity. Again, a series of three experiments had ultimately to be conducted where only one had initially been planned.

The Relay Assembly Test Room. The first of these experiments was the Relay Assembly Test Room, in which six girls (two known friends were asked to choose four other girls) were taken from their regular departments and placed in a separate test room. Although the girls were not told about it, the experimenters made sure that they obtained a record of the weekly production of each for the two weeks before her transfer, so that there would be a bench mark against which to judge the effects of subsequent experimental changes. These two weeks constituted Period I of the experiment.

At the beginning of the experiments the authors asked themselves the following six questions: (1) Do employees actually get tired out? (2) Are rest pauses desirable? (3) Is a shorter working day desirable? (4) What are the attitudes of employees toward their work and toward the company? (5) What is the effect of changing the type of working equipment? (6) Why does production fall off in the afternoon? In order to answer these questions the authors planned not only to keep an automatic record of production, but to place an observer (who later had several assistants) in the room. It was his function to keep a log of all that happened as well as to "create and maintain a friendly atmosphere in the test room" (p. 22). A daily record was constructed from the log which later became of great significance to the experiment. The girls were also given regular physical checkups; the humidity and temperature of the room were measured regularly; and during later stages of the experiment the girls were interviewed.

Before being transferred, however, the girls were asked to come to the superintendent's office. There, the purpose of the study was carefully explained to them and they were asked to work only "as they felt" (p. 21), and not to strain to produce as much as they could. Their comments were sought and some changes made in the experimenters' plans as a result. This procedure of carefully explaining changes to the girls, and of asking for and acting upon their comments, was maintained throughout the two-and-a-half years of the experiment, all in an attempt to keep their attitude constant—cooperative.

Period II of the experiment consisted of the girls' first five weeks in the test room, during which no change in hours was introduced. This enabled the experimenters to measure simply the effect of the transfer. At the beginning of Period III (which lasted for eight weeks), the six girls were taken off the departmental group incentive and were made into a separate group for payment purposes. Each girl thus received an amount more closely related to her own productivity, since under the regular system her own efforts were lost among those of the other hundred girls in the department.

The experiment proper began with Period IV during which two rest pauses, each five minutes in length, were introduced—one in the morning, one in the middle of the afternoon. In Period V, these were lengthened to ten minutes. In Period VI, six five-minute rest periods were given. In Period VII, the company provided snacks during the midmorning and midafternoon breaks.

Beginning with Period VIII, the length of the working day was changed, while the rest-period system of Period VII continued. First, work ended at 4:30 p.m. instead of at 5 p.m.; then, in Period IX, it ended at 4 o'clock. Period X was similar to Period VII in all details, but in Period XI, there was no

Saturday work. During Period XII the work schedule reverted for twelve weeks to what it had been during Periods I through III, while in Period XIII it returned to that prevailing in Periods VII and X. At the end of Period XIII the experiment had lasted for more than twenty-six months, with no experimental period (except the first) shorter than four weeks.

The outstanding result of this elaborate, and elaborately observed and measured, experiment was an almost unbroken rise, period after period, in average hourly and total weekly, productivity. In some cases this began with Period III, but it became especially pronounced after Period VII. The increase occurred despite the fact that conditions in several of the periods—for example, VII and XIII—were exactly similar; and despite the fact, also, that in Period XII the workday was drastically lengthened, so that fatigue might be expected to reduce output.

The authors then describe the changes in the relationship of the girls to each other, and in their attitudes toward the company, which had occurred concurrently with the increase in production and with the progress of the experiment. Partly through the liberal use of quotations from the girls' answers to various questions, the authors convey not only the girls' pleasure at being given rest pauses (which was only to be expected), but the fact that the girls grew more and more friendly toward each other both at work and outside. At work, they would help any girl who was not feeling well; outside work, they began meeting together for parties. That they were separated from the rest of their department and were regarded with considerable envy by their old work-mates reinforced their tendency to become a rather self-conscious "group." They expressed satisfaction at the increased freedom which they enjoyed, at being consulted instead of being merely told what to do, and at the fact that the test-room observer was much less of an invigilator than their regular supervisor, who continued to be primarily occupied with his usual duties in the main department. The girls' interest seemed to be focused as much on these changes (and on the attention paid to them by high management officials) as on changes in the length of the working day and on the introduction of rest periods per se. In sum, it was apparent that the observer (who had tried valiantly to maintain no more than a gently cooperative attitude among the girls, an attitude which would be the same at the end of the experiment as at the beginning) had neither anticipated nor been able to avoid certain dramatic and continuous changes in the total psychological climate in the test room.

Despite this very apparent intrusion of an unanticipated but highly potent variable, the authors do not ignore the possibility that the surprising increase in productivity might have been due to any one or a combination of several other factors, and they discuss the following four as most likely: (1) improved materials and methods of working; (2) the relief from fatigue provided by rest pauses and shorter working hours; (3) the reduction in monotony which might likewise be brought about by rest pauses; and (4) the effect of the changed wage incentive system.

For an answer to the first question, whether the increase in productivity could be accounted for by changes in working methods and materials, the authors refer the reader to T. N. Whitehead's detailed studies in *The Industrial Worker*. They merely summarize his work by stating that neither the preliminary studies made by the investigators nor the subsequent studies by Professor Whitehead showed any "conclusive evidence in favor of the first hypothesis" (p. 89).

The second hypothesis—that lessened fatigue might have accounted for the rise in productivity—is discussed in detail in the first half of Chapter V of *Management and the Worker*. It is rejected because both the weekly and the daily output curves of the individual operators do not behave as one would expect them to if lessened physiological fatigue were responsible for the increase in output. Fatigue, according to the authors who cite various authorities to support their reasoning, might be expected to lower production particularly toward the end of the week, and it might also be expected

11

to lower production at the end of the morning's work and at the end of the afternoon's. Since examination of the output statistics of individual operators showed that the increase in their rates of output were no greater at these than at other times of day, the authors rejected the fatigue hypothesis. Fatigue as a causal factor was, however, taken up again in connection with the other two experiments in this series and rejected far less firmly at that time.

The influence of monotony on output could similarly be tested by inspecting whether the output curves of the operators initially resembled the typical monotony curve (severe hourly fluctuations, with troughs in the middle of the morning and afternoon) and whether such resemblance lessened with the introduction of rest pauses and the shortened day. Again, examination of output statistics failed to reveal either an original monotony pattern or a subsequent disappearance of such a pattern. The monotony hypothesis was, therefore, likewise rejected.

The Second Relay Assembly Group. To assess the importance of the wage incentive factor, two entirely new experiments had to be conducted and analyzed. They are described in Chapter VI of *Management and the Worker* and consist, first, of an experiment with the so-called Second Relay Assembly Group. The workers selected for this experiment were placed next to each other, but remained in their regular departments. They were subjected to *no change* except for a change in the basis of payment exactly similar to that which the first Relay Assembly group had undergone in Period III, i.e. they were put on a small group incentive. After permitting the group to work under this incentive for some nine weeks, the operators were put back on their previous departmental incentive and observed for a further seven weeks.

Pondering the increase in output which occurred in this experiment, as it did in the first, the authors state that "in general...the findings from the Second Relay Assembly Group tended to substantiate the hypothesis that the formation of a small group for the purpose of determining piece work earnings was an important factor in the [original] Relay Assembly Test Room performance" (p. 133). In short, the sheer economic incentive effect could by no means be ignored. Because, however, the increase in production had this time been a mere 13 percent, as compared with the 30 percent increase in the Relay Assembly Test Room, the authors also conclude that the whole of the increase in the latter experiment "could not be explained in terms of this [wage incentive] factor alone" (p. 133). Indeed, explaining even the 13 percent increase was far from simple. The output of some of the operators had already shown an upward trend well before the experiment, and deliberate rivalry with the Relay Assembly Test Room (which was then in its final stages) was clearly at work during the experiment. Both these factors, rather than the changed wage incentive, could have accounted for at least a part of the increase in productivity. On the other hand, to confuse the picture still further, the Second Relay Assembly Group was regarded with jealousy by the rest of the department, and this might have kept the production of these potential isolates lower than would have been the case had they responded to the wage incentive alone.

The Mica Splitting Test Room. Concurrently with the Second Relay Assembly Group, the authors conducted the third and final study of this series, the Mica Splitting Test Room experiment. Like the Second Relay Assembly Group it, too, was designed to show that rest pauses and the complex repercussions to which they give rise have an effect on productivity independent of any changes in incentive systems. The authors now took a group of workers who were already on individual piecework (so that segregation from their department did not affect the method by which they were paid). This group was subjected to changes somewhat, but by no means completely, paralleling those of the original Relay Assembly Test Room. The lack of similarity was to be found in: (1) the fact that there were only five experimental periods instead of thirteen; (2) that each of these periods tended to be rather longer; and (3) that overtime was being worked. Each of the five periods represented an improvement in working conditions upon the period preceding it. This, of course, had not been the case in the first experiment, in which working conditions had sometimes improved, but had sometimes also worsened.

The results of the Mica Splitting Test Room were even less clear-cut than those of the other two experiments. The girls' average hourly output, after rising as anticipated, began to decline half way through the fourth period, despite the fact that their hours of work were then shorter than at any previous time. Moreover, even during the period of rising hourly production, larger differences in output between each of the girls could be noted than had existed between the girls in the Relay Assembly Test Room. The former phenomenon—that of declining average output—the authors attributed to the girls' preoccupation with the worsening employment picture at the Hawthorne plant. The great variability of the girls was regarded by the authors as but one sign of their generally lower group spirit as contrasted with that prevailing in the Relay Assembly Test Room. The girls never regarded themselves as "special" and as separate from the rest of their department to the same extent as did the girls in the Relay Assembly Test Room, nor did they establish such close personal relations. The greater heterogeneity of these girls' backgrounds (a wider range in age and ethnic origin) seems to have been one reason for this; another was the fact that the rest of their department underwent changes in hours and length of working week similar to theirs, at least from Period IV onward. Moreover, working as they did on individual piece rates, the girls had less incentive to help each other and to draw close to each other.

The authors' summary of the two experiments which grew out of the original Relay Assembly Test Room was, then, to note that the wage incentive factor alone could not explain the continuous increase in output in the Relay Assembly Test Room and, second, that even such effects as could be attributed to wage incentives were highly dependent on other factors so that "it was impossible to consider [a wage incentive system] as a thing in itself having an independent effect on the individual" (p. 160).

Results of the Rest Pause Experiments. The interpretation of the three experiments as a whole is given in Chapters VII and VIII of *Management and the Worker*. The authors came out of their deliberations still considerably confused. In part, they were ready to attribute the results of the original Relay Assembly Test Room *quite specifically to the changed supervision* introduced by the investigators. By convincing the employees that their jobs and bonuses were secure, and by allowing them to participate in an ever changing experiment in which they alone were involved, the investigators and (without being desirous to do so) the observer-"supervisor" had profoundly altered the total social situation for the operators in the Relay Assembly Test Room. This situation, the authors now realized, was so complex that it could not be described in terms of isolated variables, but "needed to be described and understood as a system of interdependent elements" (p. 183).

At the core of this "system," however, they saw not the specific factor of supervision, but the *more general and vague factor of the employees' "attitudes and preoccupations"* (p. 184), and about these they could say very little that was specific at this point. Management, looking at the experiments from a practical point of view, might have regarded the case in favor of rest pauses as sufficiently proven to introduce them in the regular shop departments. It also gained a generally "improved understanding of many of its problems" (p. 185). But from a researcher's point of view, the results had essentially been confusing and negative. The authors, surveying all the information at their disposal, were ultimately unwilling to attribute such results as they had obtained to anything specific—supervision included. The authors felt that the questions raised could only be answered by a systematic study of employees' attitudes.

15

Part II: The Analysis of Complaints

Part II of the book, therefore, developed out of Part I. Although entitled "A Plan for the Improvement of Employee Relations," it may be seen as the authors' initial essay at a study of attitudes. It contains an account of the development of an extensive employee-interview program, the data from which, so the authors hoped, would shed light both on the development of attitudes and on the influence of attitudes upon output. The program was begun when the Relay Assembly Test Room experiment had run half its course; it originally encompassed one staff department only, but was later expanded to cover the entire Operating Branch.

The program had at the start been designed quite independently of the Relay Assembly Test Room experiment. Its purpose had been to supply case material for supervisory training courses. Such courses were already standard at Hawthorne and existed chiefly to teach the company's rules and policies to new supervisors. The interviewing program represents the authors' efforts to teach supervisors something about the employees' point of view. We shall not describe in detail the various methods, imaginative though they were for that time, used by the authors in these training programs, nor the employees' and the supervisors' reaction to them. It may be noted in passing that there is no evidence whatever that supervisors learned in these courses how to manipulate employees to the latters' detriment. On the contrary, at least some of the supervisors felt "up in the air" and dissatisfied (p. 218) because they had not been given definitive answers to their problems, even though most of those involved—both supervisors and workers—felt enthusiastic about the program and the company's interest in their fate which it seemed to indicate. In the light of the Test Room studies, however, the authors hoped that the data obtained from the interviews would prove useful not only as training material but, as stated above, that they would shed light on the influence that attitudes might have on operator performance.

A painstaking analysis was, therefore, made (Chapter XI)

of the more than 86,000 comments made on 80 topics during some 10,000 interviews. Comments on any one topic were added together and the ratio of the total number of such comments to the total number of interviews was used as an index of the "urgency" of that topic. (This index, the authors themselves admit, was considerably less revealing than it might have been, since one person who was completely, but uniquely, preoccupied with a topic could increase the ratio by as much as many persons each of whom might have offered but a few comments on that topic.) A ratio of the number of favorable comments on any one topic to the total number of comments on that topic was also calculated, and taken as an index of the feelings—favorable, neutral, or unfavorable—which employees had on that topic. This was called the "tone" of the topic. These ratios were calculated separately for men and women for all 80 topics.

Comparison between the two groups showed that they differed in urgency rather than in tone. In particular, men showed a more lively interest in matters affecting their own and their families' economic security (pensions and employment) than did women, while women were the more sensitive to working conditions—overtime, fatigue, social contact.

In the course of time, however, the authors became convinced that more meaningful material would be obtained if employees were not guided to talk about a predetermined range of topics, but were encouraged to talk freely about any topic in which they were interested. The statistical analysis of comments made on any one topic revealed a tremendous amount of variation between the reaction of different individuals, making generalizations about how workers felt on that topic almost meaningless. At the same time, the authors were struck by the fact that any individual's comments made much greater sense when taken, not in conjunction with others' comments on the same topic, but in conjunction with his own comments and expressions of feelings on other topics. The authors became increasingly aware that the nature of the comments they were eliciting—in terms of both frequency and urgency—were understandable only if the expectations and moods of the person concerned, and not alone the objective situation facing him, were taken into account. Thus the same topic, e.g. advancement, might elicit widely varying reactions not only because, objectively, opportunities for advancement differed from one person to the next, but also because different people approach an objectively similar promotion situation with different expectations about how fast they ought to and need to advance. Also accounting for wide variations in the tone of comments made on certain topics was the fact that some topics seemed to lend themselves particularly well to the expression of current, more general states of satisfaction or dissatisfaction. Company cafeteria facilities, for example, are traditionally used for the release of generally accumulated hostilities. The cause of such feelings may be too vague to result in comments which are specifically appropriate, or the individual may be unwilling to enlarge upon the cause even though he is fully aware of it. Since these more general states of satisfaction and dissatisfaction are often widely shared by members of some groups, and since they are often related to social relationships between groups within the plant, the authors refer to them as "social sentiments."

The authors, therefore, concluded that further exploration of employee attitudes on specific topics required a more detailed study of these more general social sentiments and their interrelation with other factors. To such a study, Part III of the book is devoted. It is entitled "A Conceptual Scheme for the Understanding of Employee Dissatisfactions," since the authors wished more and more to emphasize the interrelated nature of the phenomena with which they were dealing. Hence the word "scheme"—although the use of the word "conceptual" is more open to question.

Part III: Understanding Employee Attitudes

This part of the book begins with a more detailed and specific explanation of what the authors mean when they describe some comments—complaints, in particular—as being based on sentiment. The authors note first that complaints referring to persons and policies were far more frequent than they had anticipated. Moreover, there seemed to be an inherent and very important difference between this type of complaint and complaints referring to working conditions. The latter involved physical, sensory processes, which could be verified by the use of objective, physical operations of measurement. The former, on the other hand, inevitably involved the use of subjective, psychological "yardsticks," on the precision and relevance of which there may be a great deal of disagreement. When a person complains that a certain wage rate is unduly low, he may be making that judgment in the light of what he thinks is due the kind of *person* performing that work, e.g. a married man. Others may regard the same rate as not unreasonable in view of the kind of *work* it is. The authors' argument is that the matter must be regarded as one of sentiment in the sense that there is no objective way (no way external to some person's judgment) of measuring how much money is due what kind of person (or kind of work).

Having tied simple, manifest complaints to more complex sentiments latent within the individual, the authors proceed to describe the special interview method which they evolved in order to elicit latent material of this kind, material about "the emotional significance to the worker of particular events and objects in his experience." The rules for conducting this kind of interview, and the "rules of orientation" (p. 273) used to interpret the material obtained, bear a striking resemblance to those used in nondirective counseling.[3] They make highly instructive reading even today, and they were effective enough at the time to enable the authors to delve quite deeply into the personal histories and preoccupations of some of their informants.

[3]This method of counseling grew up completely independently of the Hawthorne Studies, and probably subsequent to them. Its originator, Carl Rogers, was a psychologist working largely in the student clinic of the University of Chicago. His first major work on the topic, *Counseling and Psychotherapy*, was not published until 1942. It contains several explicit compliments on the pioneering efforts of Roethlisberger and Dickson.

The analysis of these interviews, as distinct from the earlier ones which had been analyzed complaint by complaint, again took the authors only one step farther toward their goal. These interviews brought out the extent to which an individual's behavior at work depended on his personal situation outside work: his family problems, his personal aspirations, his background and upbringing. While the authors were willing to devote one chapter to this relationship between attitudes toward work and the worker's situation outside the plant, they conclude by warning against overemphasizing that relationship and stress that various aspects of the immediate work situation itself are probably even more important in determining attitudes toward work. The authors admittedly regarded some of the workers' reactions as "obsessive" and to that extent pathological, but they explicitly put the blame for this on the work situation, not on the individual's sick personality. The final diagrammatic "scheme" drawn up by the authors for interpreting complaints and reduced work effectiveness (p. 327) therefore places as much emphasis on social and physical conditions in the work situation as on the individual's personal history and his situation outside the plant. The social, not the psychological, context of complaints was now of prime importance to the authors (p. 374).

The second half of Part III, beginning with Chapter XV, is therefore devoted to an exploration by means of interviews of what in the work situation itself leads individuals to perceive it in the way they do. This time, however, the authors talked not with workers but with supervisors from various levels of the supervisory structure. With the help of these interviews, the authors were able to understand better the stresses and strains, as well as the satisfactions, associated with various supervisory positions. Their analysis of the position of the assistant foreman may be cited as an example. The assistant foreman was regarded as well above the level of the section and group chief and, for that reason, was cut off from them and, by implication, cut off from the working staff in general. Yet he was still only on the periphery of "real executive rank"

(p. 370). The strains of such a marginal position are fully described. These chapters also deal with the manner in which individual differences among group and section chiefs in attitudes toward very similar (namely, poor) advancement possibilities are linked to differences in social background, experience, and individual aspirations. There are, in this part of the book, other insights into the social system of the modern factory, both as regards its authority structure and its other divisions such as those of occupation, age, and sex. Indeed, this most neglected part of the book is, in many ways, one of its very richest.

Chapter XV is, unintentionally, also a rather amusing one, because of the section on the attitudes of group and section chiefs to the operators directly under their supervision. It is apparent that even in the twenties, and even before training, many of the supervisors already had a "new conception of leadership," at least at the verbal level. This new conception had all the paraphernalia of "saying a cheery word" to the operators, "selling yourself," and even "listening to their grievances and allowing them to express their own ideas"! While on the one hand adding reinforcement to Gilson's criticism that anyone halfway familiar with industry knew and practiced the authors' supposed preachings long before the authors themselves discovered their text, these statements from the mouths of the supervisors also make it apparent that "human relating" in the epithetic sense was not invented by the university professor but was in existence long before his advent on the industrial scene.

In any case, the result of these further probes into attitudes was to lead the authors back into the plant in their search for causal variables.

Part IV: Common Environment and Group Formation

The authors re-entered the plant apparently impressed by two facts. First, they had learned from the interviews of supervisors (described in the last chapters of Part III) that it would be more fruitful to look for causal variables of attitudes not in that which was unique in each person's situation, but in that part of fate which he shared with groups of others. It should be noted, however, that at the end of these studies of attitudes, the authors generally thought of "a group" as a class of individuals (e.g. all higher supervisors, all lower supervisors; all office workers and all shop operators), and not as individuals conscious of themselves as a group or at least in regular relationship with each other. To investigate how a shared environment affected such groups was therefore the authors' aim in the fourth part of the book.

There is a second major lesson which seems to have impressed itself on the authors as a result of the studies incorporated in Parts II and III. That lesson was in the realm of methodology and involved relinquishing reliance on interviewing as the chief research technique in favor of combined observation and interviewing, with observation as the senior partner. It is interesting to note that the transition from Part I of the book to Part II, when the authors had ceased to look for causal variables in the physical environment and began to search for them in the attitudes of individuals, was also marked by a change in methodology. From measuring output, the researchers had turned to interviewing. Now, having shifted their emphasis from the individual to the group, they at the same time changed their methodology once more, this time from interviewing to observation. The authors' growing recognition of the complexity of the situation which they were trying to analyze seems to have led them to adopt a research method in which their own role became increasingly passive. Foregoing both the arbitrariness inherent in the introduction of experimental variables and the equal arbitrariness involved in taking someone from his place of work in order to interview him, the authors seem to have decided that meaningful data could only be gathered from a group of persons in a setting to which they were accustomed. It was for this reason that they set up the Bank Wiring Observation Room.

The Bank Wiring Observation Room. This study is the best known of the various studies included in *Management and the Worker.* It is the study in which is discussed—among many other topics—the now well-known phenomenon of group control of individual output. The researchers had become aware of this phenomenon as soon as the interview program (partly as an economy measure, partly as a result of the change in research orientation already discussed) began to concentrate on small working groups instead of picking isolated individuals from various and scattered departments. These localized interviews already had begun to reveal that incentive plans were not working as management expected, because groups evolved production standards to which individuals were forced to adhere—and supervisors could do nothing about it and were intensely disliked if they tried. Informal leaders seemed to exist in these groups who handled "external relations" (i.e. relations with supervisors, engineers, and inspectors) and who taught newcomers how to dissemble before such prying outsiders. The Bank Wiring Observation Room study was, therefore, planned both "to develop the new [observation] method" and "to obtain more exact information about social groups within the company" (p. 385).

The authors, as always, describe carefully: (1) their reasons for studying one small group intensively rather than merging superficial observations from various groups in the hope that a meaningful composite would result; (2) their reasons for segregating the group from its regular department; and (3) their reasons for selecting operators engaged in wiring and soldering so-called "banks" of terminals. The study was introduced to department supervisors, to foremen, and to the fourteen operators who really constituted the bank wiremen in the same deliberate way as the other studies had been. Once again, observations were made during a base period before the operators knew that they were to be studied, and careful note was taken of the fact that the group, in its new environment and in the presence of the observer, did not settle down to its normal behavior for some two or three weeks. The study lasted from November 1931 to May 1932 when it had to be discontinued because of lack of work. During the course of the study, the investigators initiated no changes. It is clear, however, that the group must have been operating in a climate of growing uncertainty over their jobs, since from January on the men were put on progressively shorter hours, and later on a reduced work week, and finally to working on alternating weeks (p. 425). We shall refer in Chapter IV below to the authors' remarkable failure to draw much attention to this fact while at least presenting the reader with enough data to draw his own conclusions.

The first of the chapters describing the results of the Bank Wiring Observation Room deals in great detail with the output situation. It was apparent that the operators had only a partial understanding of the mechanics of the incentive system under which they were supposedly working. It was also apparent that, contrary to management's expectations, there was a widely held view among the operators that the wiring of two banks (a total of 6,000—6,600 terminals) constituted "a day's work." Exceeding this rate would, it was believed, be dangerous in some way which the operators could only vaguely specify: dangerous to the individual and, even more, dangerous to the rest of the department. Official production records showed that these opinions had a definite influence on behavior: most of the individuals had so-called "straight-line" output curves; their reported weekly average hourly output showed little change from one week to the next and was in fact around two banks a day. This was achieved by under- or, more usually, overreporting actual output, and by all sorts of other subterfuges, such as claiming more or less time for "day work" than was justified ("day work" was time which would not enter into the calculation of the individual's average hourly production for that week). Further analysis—now of actual, not officially reported, production—showed that only three of the nine wiremen produced as much as they claimed; some consistently produced *less* than they claimed, but one produced more.

So far, analysis had taken each individual in isolation. Inspection of data bearing on output quality revealed, how-

24

ever, that the charging of some types of defects was very much within the discretion of the inspector (as contrasted with other kinds of defects which were capable of being established by entirely objective means), and that one of the inspectors not only found more of the former types of defects than did the other inspectors but that he would charge some of the solder-men or wiremen with them to a greater extent than others. This was reciprocated by the operators concerned, who charged more "day work allowance" against this inspector than against the others. By such means, the investigators were able to gain a first approximation of some of the personal relationships in the room.

Puzzled by what appeared to be unchecked offenses against company rules, the authors began a more thorough study of another set of relationships, that between supervisors and operators in the Bank Wiring Observation Room. They found that first and even second level supervisors (group and section chiefs) were regarded by the employees very much as one of themselves. Only assistant foremen and up were regarded with anything approaching respect. Group and section chiefs in turn did not wholeheartedly identify with management and its rules. On the contrary, placed as they were in a compromising position by being observers of breaches of rules, dependent on the good will of the men, and not really powerful enough to control them, they tended to side with them. Consequently, they gave a highly selective picture of conditions in the Bank Wiring Observation Room to their superiors. The chain of upward communication had clearly snapped between the section chief and the assistant foreman.

After some vignettes of the individuals involved in this final study (vignettes which leave one feeling that this was a rather slaphappy, not overly mature group of individuals), the authors begin to trace the relationships between the operators themselves. The web of these personal relationships was found to be very intricate. Despite beliefs about production which were shared by and which united the group as a whole, the operators were at the same time split into subgroups. This could be seen not only in such workaday matters as who traded jobs with whom, but extended even to such esoteric matters as differences in topics deemed suitable for lunchtime conversation, and even to differences in the quantity and quality of candy eaten! On the whole, the more serious-minded subgroup, and the one which considered itself superior, was the one containing individuals whose actual output, and whose reported output, conformed most closely to what all agreed was the desired norm. Individuals in the second subgroup, regarded by the other subgroup as having less prestige than themselves, produced less than the agreed-upon norm, but reported more than they produced. Those individuals who conformed least to the norms of the group as a whole (whether in these matters of output, in their relations with supervisors, or in their relations with other group members) were most severely excluded from the group's (or groups') relationships and were punished in other ways for their nonconformity. Conformity and nonconformity to the norms, rather than location in the room or occupational status, seemed to determine whether or not an operator was accepted or rejected by the group.

The authors conclude their description of the Bank Wiring Observation Room with a discussion of the possible reasons that such an elaborate group structure in general, and output control in particular, should have existed. After debating various alternative explanations—including the effects on the group of being observed (pp. 526–531)—the authors propose their own analysis. We shall discuss this analysis in greater detail in Chapter IV of this monograph. Suffice it to say that the authors' explanation is cast in terms of the wiremen's position in the plant as a whole relative to other groups—particularly their standing relative to, and their working relationships with, technologists and supervisors. The chapter in which this analysis occurs is extremely important and contains most of the authors' explanatory theory. With this analysis ends the description of the empirical work which constituted the bulk of the Hawthorne Studies. No link of unresolved scientific problems ties this part to the following, and final, part of the book.

Part V: Applications

The fifth and final part of the book, entitled "Applications to Practice of Research Results," is the shortest, its three chapters comprising fewer than sixty pages. The first of these chapters reviews the basic concepts used in the book: technical and human organization, formal and informal organization, the logic of sentiments and of cost. We shall not describe what the authors mean by these concepts. They are basic to, though not exhaustive of, all sociological thinking about organizations. To do them full justice would take us beyond the main purpose of this monograph. The second chapter is again little more than a restatement of the authors' analysis, although this time a restatement of its implications for management activities in such areas as the introduction of technological change. The final chapter spells out the implications which the authors see for personnel administration in particular. In these last fourteen pages of the book is described the Hawthorne "counseling program," which was instituted some five years after the termination of the Hawthorne Studies proper.

These, then, are the Hawthorne Studies on which Mayo based his three well-known analyses of industrial civilization.[4] It is these studies, and Mayo's analyses of them, which have been subjected to so much criticism.

[4]Elton Mayo, *The Human Problems of an Industrial Civilization* (New York: The Macmillan Co., 1933); *The Social Problems of an Industrial Civilization,* (Boston: Graduate School of Business Administration, Harvard University, 1946); *The Political Problems of an Industrial Civilization* (Boston: Graduate School of Business Administration, Harvard University, 1947).

⊹ CHAPTER III ⊹

Criticisms of the Mayo School

READERS interested in the study of industrial relations will be familiar with the several and repeated criticisms[1] directed at the "human relations in industry" branch of industrial sociology and at "the Harvard group," for both of which the late Elton Mayo is designated the leader. One is tempted to remark that among a large number of sociologists and econ-

[1] The criticisms to which reference is made appear in the following:

ARTICLES:

Michael Argyle, "The Relay Assembly Test Room in Retrospect," *Occupational Psychology,* Vol. 27, 1953, pp. 98–103.

Daniel Bell, "Adjusting Men to Machines," *Commentary,* Vol. 3, 1947, pp. 79–88.

Reinhard Bendix and Lloyd N. Fisher, "The Perspectives of Elton Mayo," *Review of Economics and Statistics,* Vol. 31, 1949, pp. 312–321.

V. W. Bladen, "Economics and Human Relations," *Canadian Journal of Economics and Political Science,* Vol. 14, 1948, pp. 301–311.

Herbert Blumer, "Sociological Theory in Industrial Relations," *American Sociological Review,* Vol. 12, 1947, pp. 271–278.

John T. Dunlop, "Framework for the Analysis of Industrial Relations: Two Views," *Industrial and Labor Relations Review,* Vol. 3, 1950, pp. 383–393.

Ellis Freeman, *Social Psychology* (New York: Henry Holt Co., 1936), Chapters 18 and 19, pp. 323–366.

Georges Friedmann, "Philosophy Underlying the Hawthorne Investigations," *Social Forces,* Vol. 28, 1949, pp. 204–209; trans. by W. J. Goode and H. L. Sheppard, from *Problèmes Humaines du Machinisme Industriel* (Paris: Gallimard, 1947), pp. 300–309.

C. W. M. Hart, "Industrial Relations Research and Social Theory," *Canadian Journal of Economics and Political Science,* Vol. 15, 1949, pp. 53–73.

Clark Kerr, "What Became of the Independent Spirit?" *Fortune,* Vol. 48, 1953, pp. 110–111 et. seq.

John B. Knox, "Sociological Theory and Industrial Sociology," *Social Forces,* Vol. 33, 1955, pp. 240–244.

omists, "taking a shot at Mayo"—and at human relations—seems to be a favored pastime of several years' standing. A facetious response, while merited by the repetition and lack of originality of much of the criticism is, however, not in keeping with the seriousness of some of the charges and the earnestness with which they are made.

Because critics of the Mayo school see its writings as constituting an interlocking ideology, their criticisms have in turn been highly interrelated. Nevertheless, it is possible to distinguish four somewhat separate areas of criticism. The first and most basic criticism takes issue with the group's view of modern society as one in a condition of "anomie" (i.e. made up of morally confused, isolated individuals surrounded by a society disorganized and full of conflict). The Mayo group is said to regard modern society as a mere leftover after the breakup of group solidarity in the old established

W. A. Koivisto, "Value, Theory, and Fact in Industrial Sociology," *American Journal of Sociology*, Vol. 58, 1953, pp. 564–572.

C. Wright Mills, "The Contributions of Sociology to Studies of Industrial Relations," *Proceedings of the First Annual Meeting*, Industrial Relations Research Association, Vol. 1, 1948, pp. 199–222.

Wilbert E. Moore, "Current Issues in Industrial Sociology," *American Sociological Review*, Vol. 12, 1947, pp. 651–657; "Industrial Sociology: Status and Prospects," *American Sociological Review*, Vol. 13, 1948, pp. 382–400.

E. V. Schneider, "Limitations on Observation in Industrial Sociology," *Social Forces,* Vol. 28, 1950, pp. 279–284.

Louis Schneider, "An Industrial Sociology—For What Ends?" *Antioch Review*, Vol. 10, 1950, pp. 407–417.

Harold L. Sheppard, "The Social and Historical Philosophy of Elton Mayo," *Antioch Review*: Vol. 10, 1950, pp. 396–406; "The Treatment of Unionism in 'Managerial Sociology,'" *American Sociological Review*, Vol. 14, 1949, pp. 310–313.

R. C. Sorenson, "The Concept of Conflict in Industrial Sociology," *Social Forces*, Vol. 29, 1951, pp. 263–267.

R. C. Stone, "Conflicting Approaches to the Study of Worker-Management Relations," *Social Forces*, Vol. 31, 1952, pp. 117–124.

BOOK REVIEWS:

Mary Gilson, "Review of Roethlisberger and Dickson, *Management and the Worker*," in *American Journal of Sociology*, Vol. 46, 1940, pp. 98–101.

Robert S. Lynd, "Review of Whitehead, *Leadership in a Free Society*," in *Political Science Quarterly*, Vol. 52, 1937, pp. 590–592.

Ordway Tead, "Review of Mayo's *Social Problems of an Industrial Civilization*," in *Survey Graphic*, Vol. 35, 1946, pp. 179–180.

societies, and to see industrial workers as social beings who continue to harbor an ancient need for submerging themselves in the purposes of a larger group in order to find freedom. As a solution to the problems of modern society, the Mayo group is said to propose reclaiming of individual and society through industrial organizations, so managed that there is spontaneous collaboration for a common purpose.[2]

This faulty view of society, according to the critics, results in three further errors or deficiencies in the assumptions, evaluations, and recommendations of the group: (1) an image of the worker which reflects both the acceptance of management's goals and its view of workers, coupled with a willingness to manipulate workers for management's ends; (2) failure to pay attention to methods of accommodating industrial conflict, such as collective bargaining; and (3) a specific failure to take unions into account.

Social Change and Anomie

The most far-reaching charge against the Mayo group in particular and against the human relations group in general is that of inadequate conceptualization of the major problems in industrial relations. This is due to a logically prior inadequate view of the development of anomie in modern society (to which we have already referred briefly). Specifically, the critics point out, the group has failed to recognize the problem of conflict and conflicting interests of the parties in industrial relations and has therefore failed to look for the causes as well as the implications of this conflict. As a consequence the energy, attention, and enthusiasm of the group have been directed toward concepts and phenomena which are, by comparison, superficial and even trivial: status strivings of employees, relationships in informal groups in the factory, the need for catharsis through a counselor, and improving "communications," for example.

Kerr is one of the most distinguished as well as one of the most vehement critics of the Mayo ideology. Speaking as a

[2]Such a summary of the ideology of the Mayo school is given by Clark Kerr in his article, *loc. cit.*, pp. 111 and 134. Mayo's own views on modern society are to be found in the books cited in n. 4, p. 27, above.

liberal economist he takes issue with the human relations school because of his very different evaluation of many characteristics of today's society. Far from deploring the breaking up of group solidarity, Kerr believes that "in the division of loyalties...to self, to family, to state, to union...is seen the guarantee of freedom."[3] Rather than deploring competition, he is happy that today's society "is a society of accommodated conflict rather than universal collaboration."[4] In this concern for encouraging the independence of man, he is against any organization's having an increased control over man's loyalties because this is a move in a totalitarian direction. He states: "We cannot accept the view that rationality and initiative are vouchsafed only to the elite, and that to the common man is left only the virtues of faith and obedience...."[5]

Bendix and Fisher, in an earlier article, had taken issue with Mayo's ideology on grounds similar to those of Kerr, although they outline a position somewhat to his left. They examined the reasons for the fundamental failure to deal with conflict, and their conclusion was that they lie in Mayo's own feelings on the subject. "It is difficult to understand Mayo's work unless one realizes how much he abhors conflict, competition, or disagreement: conflict to him is a 'social disease' and cooperation is 'social health.'"[6] Conflict between the parties in industrial relations is more deeply rooted and a larger matter than Mr. Mayo wishes to see it. "The Goliath of industrial warfare cannot be slain by the David of human relations.... It is the peculiar blindness of Mr. Mayo and others who have seen the medieval vision, that they do not understand that it is precisely the *freedom* to conflict which establishes the boundaries within which the actual conflict can be contained."[7] They note, too, that Mayo had a tendency to "seek to prove too much" and to override existing facts in his enthusiasm for his own approach and solutions. They disagree particularly with the Mayo view that cooperation must be, as they put it, "traditional rather than deliberate,

[3]*Loc. cit.*, p. 134.   [6]*Loc. cit.*, p. 272.
[4]*Ibid.*   [7]*Ibid.*, p. 318.
[5]*Ibid.*

spontaneous rather than voluntary,"[8] and state that in advocating this kind of relationship for modern industry "Mr. Mayo assumes what he has yet to prove: that there is a natural community between worker and manager."[9] They believe that the humanitarian role outlined for the managerial elite in the Mayo system is actually an impossibility, "the implicit denial of the inevitably authoritarian aspects of a factory system plays a strategic role in Mr. Mayo's philosophy."[10]

Sheppard finds the Mayo analysis in general, and the concept of "spontaneous collaboration" in particular, to be inadequate and unsuited to the real nature of society's problems:

> In all of the Mayo group's emphasis on collaboration and solidarity, there is no consideration of the political and economic problems that might be expected to be relevant to the achievement of spontaneous collaboration, nor any consideration of the goals toward which men might cooperate, nor any attention given to the relative roles of various social classes that would participate under such conditions of collaboration. Also conspicuously lacking is an interest in *conflict, classes* or *interest* groups.[11]

Blumer addresses himself to the problem of evaluating the concepts and theories which students of industrial relations have employed for their task, and he finds the human relations group (as well as others) sadly wanting. His observations are that "the most noteworthy feature of the relations between workers and management in American industry is that the relations are dynamic, uncrystallized, changing...[and] in a state of continuous tension."[12] He adds that "fundamentally, workers and managers in our economy are necessarily in conflict with each other,"[13] and "industrial relations are becoming increasingly a matter of alignment of organizations."[14] In the face of these developments, to approach indus-

[8]*Ibid.*, p. 315.
[9]*Ibid.*, p. 317.
[10]*Ibid.*, p. 316.
[11]"The Social and Historical Philosophy of Elton Mayo," *loc. cit.*, p. 399.
[12]*Loc. cit.*, p. 272.
[13]*Ibid.*, p. 273.
[14]*Ibid.*, p. 276.

trial relations as one would study a primitive tribe, "as if they were expressions of a body of established recognitions or definitions...misses [their] central character...."[15] Similarly, "the promise that industrial relations are primarily a structure of stratified status relationships" Blumer cannot see as "meaningful when applied to the relations between workers and management."[16] These two criticisms apply to the human relations approach as well as his observation that the importance of direct relations between the people in the local plant or factory diminishes before the organizational relationships. While he acknowledges the necessity for the "intimate familiarity" which researchers have cultivated, he thinks this must be combined with a "broad imaginative grasp" which has so far been lacking.

Bell, too, has noted: "There is no view of the larger institutional framework of our economic system within which these relationships arise and have their meaning."[17] He surveys those developments of the past two decades in this country which the Mayo researchers have failed to take into account, and contends that they have continued to apply a theoretical system "taken over from Pareto" in which "all action is defined in terms of equilibrium." He doubts whether "such a mechanical analogy is truly enlightening for the analysis of dynamic structures."[18] Among important developments in what he calls "the profound social revolution" is "a new class structure," in which the technical and managerial employees have ascended as technology has advanced, while within the working class skilled work has decreased and "a general class of semi-skilled machine tenders" has been created. The social mobility picture has been changed because "these new technical-managerial jobs require a degree of skill that is attainable only by long education."[19] Consequently, "The insecurity of the skill-less in a world that increasingly uses skill as the basis of reward is now the chief fact in the life of the masses, and the worker tends more and more to base his attitudes on the assumption that he—and his son—will remain in the

---

[15]*Ibid.*, p. 274.
[16]*Ibid.*
[17]*Loc. cit.*, p. 86.

[18]*Ibid.*, p. 87.
[19]*Ibid.*, p. 86.

working class."[20] Bell suggests that one might question what is emerging from this process—perhaps "the development of certain types of militancy among workers," perhaps "the beginnings of an elite psychology in the technical-managerial group."[21]

It is this kind of analysis, Bell feels, which reveals "more basic conflicts between worker and management" than have been envisioned by those studies which have "rested on the assumption that better face-to-face relationships between management and union, and management and worker, would lead to peace."[22]

Sorenson is another who takes issue with the Mayo group on the matter of their view of conflict in industrial relations. He observes: "The emergence of strong unionism introduced conflict to the industrial scene once dominated by a stronger capital.... Worker consent has emerged...as a basis for consent which must be persuaded and won, not ordered or assumed."[23] Rather than agreeing with the fundamentalists (of the Mayo group) that "conflict need not exist today," Sorenson says that, favor or oppose it, conflict is present in our society. "To postulate the identical interests of man is to deny the division of labor and to assume an absolute constancy of social progress."[24] And further, their conflict itself contributes to a realistic collaboration between labor and management. He cites Simmel's statement: "Without the conflict of opposition there would result an accommodative relationship spelling subordination rather than eventual agreement."[25]

That Mayo did not have an adequate understanding of modern society has been ascribed by some of his critics to his failure to use an appropriate sociological method or theory —or indeed any sociological method or theory, whether appropriate or not. Hart, for example, states that although the Mayo group talks about the theories of, and expresses indebtedness to the ideas of, sociologists Durkheim and Pareto, it is the individualistic theory of Freud which they have actually

[20]*Ibid.*, p. 87.
[21]*Ibid.*
[22]*Ibid.*, p. 84.

[23]*Loc. cit.*, p. 263.
[24]*Ibid.*, p. 264.
[25]*Ibid.*, p. 266.

followed. "Despite the elaborate lip service paid to 'collective representations' in the theory, in the empirical research attention is confined to individual representations and hence the empirical data too often appear to be a contribution to psychiatry rather than sociology."[26] Moore also deplores the discrepancy between their theories and their methods of investigation. He points out that hypotheses and analytical problems are not made explicit, and that the descriptive techniques they employed lend themselves least well to testing the theories in which they purported to be interested.[27] He argues that real sociology is needed and notes that often the researchers have not been sociologists. "It is not wholly surprising, therefore, to find the sociologically obvious reported with an air of breathless discovery, as in the case of the Western Electric researchers who took several years to find that the individual reacts selectively to his environment in terms of his definition of the situation."[28]

Image of the Worker

An imposing number of critics, representing several different points of view, have attacked the view of workers offered by Mayo and his followers. A psychologist, Freeman, one of the first to criticize, sees a clash between modern man and industrial work, and would agree with Mayo that the submergence of the self is necessary if the worker is to achieve psychological satisfaction in a modern factory. "The primitive would be better adapted psychologically for industrial tasks, if he could be maintained in his pristine state of social solidarity."[29] His point of difference with Mayo, however, is a fundamental one since, as he sees it, civilized man in becoming

[26]*Loc. cit.*, p. 56.

[27]Moore perhaps pays a backhanded compliment to the Hawthorne Studies when he argues for the employment of other and more rigorous methods of investigation. "Experimental procedures seem to have been rejected largely because the early experiments in the Western Electric study were sociologically naive. This has led the group primarily influenced by that experience to a radical rejection of careful observational controls in favor of the most primitive methods of gathering information." "Current Issues in Industrial Sociology," *loc. cit.*, n., p. 653.

[28]*Ibid.*, p. 657.

[29]*Op. cit.*, Chapter 18, "Industrial Cooperation," p. 340.

civilized has developed away from the capacity so to submerge himself and "possesses urges which are not alone social but anti-social and egotistical to a degree absent in savages."[30] And, consequently, "The antagonism between submergence of the self and individuation in civilized man must be taken as a base-line datum in dealing with the problem."[31] For this reason, Freeman's conclusions are very different from Mayo's. "When we set industrial cooperation against a larger psychological background than that of profit and earning a living alone we cannot escape the fact that it offends as well as serves civilized man. . . ."[32] Therefore: "Because it operates under conditions of competition for profit, industry today could not, with the best will in the world, offer the ameliorations which would make the rigors of the division of labor tolerable."[33]

Further charges against the human relations group are that its view of workers suspiciously shadows that of management and that the methods the group has devised and the advice it gives are designed to manipulate workers for management's purposes. According to Freeman, "Mayo has made it a principle to contemplate the individual as a whole, but it must be confessed, only as a producing unit and not as a living unit,"[34] and "Mayo has developed methods of interviewing and of estimating personal qualities, that may eventually become very effective in adapting personnel to maximum output. The only danger is that some might consider these methods as a contribution to the welfare of the worker."[35]

The accusation of Koivisto is that "the individual is not seen as a goal-setting or goal-achieving creature. Rather, he is considered as an inert 'element' that does not act unless acted upon and to be manipulated by means of human relations 'skills.'"[36]

Mills notes "latent images" in the writings of Mayo and his colleagues which suggest to him "a technicalization of the manager and a sentimentalization of the employee."[37] And he

[30]*Ibid.*, p. 338. [32]*Ibid.*, p. 324.
[31]*Ibid.*, p. 337. [33]*Ibid.*, p. 334.
[34]*Ibid.*, in Chapter 19, "Industrial Efficiency," p. 360.
[35]*Ibid.* [37]*Loc. cit.*, p. 209.
[36]*Loc. cit.*, p. 570.

poses the question: "How much of the advice, given and latent, can be picked up with the simple formula: to make the worker happy, efficient, and cooperative we need only make the managers intelligent, rational, knowing? Is this the latent political formula of human relations research?"[38] Mills charges that the attention paid to the informal groups among workers is a technique of manipulation, and his paraphrase of advice from Whitehead is: "To secure the spontaneous, efficient collaboration of his workers, the manager must pay attention to their informal relations, and seek to gain acceptance in some way among these informal groups."[39] The counseling program for the workers in a factory, Mills refers to as "an institutionalization within industry of manipulation."[40] Schneider has a similar interpretation.

> Industrial sociology...may be seen as a somewhat elaborate and subtle device for better control of the human materials of industry. Coercion would be replaced by a kind of limited psychiatric hearing for worker grievances, in line both with the Mayo group's concern with psychopathology in industry and its emphasis on a managerial perspective. Direct, angry exhortation not to "loaf on the job" would be made unnecessary by the indirect but effective compulsions coming from informally organized working groups possessed of "high morale." The wild worker-animal would approach the state of domestication.[41]

The criticism from Bell on this point is also sharp.

> The gravest charge that can be leveled against these researches is that they uncritically accept industry's own conception of workers as a *means* to be manipulated or adjusted to impersonal ends. The belief in man as an end in himself has been ground under by the machine, and the social science of the factory researchers is not a science of man, but a cow-sociology. Burleigh Gardner has written: "The more satisfied (the worker) is, the greater will be his self-esteem, the more content he will be, and, therefore, the more efficient in what he is doing." Surely this is a fitting

[38]*Ibid.*, p. 218.   [40]*Ibid.*
[39]*Ibid.*, p. 215.   [41]Louis Schneider, *loc. cit.*, p. 409.

inscription to go under the Model T symbol of Huxley's *Brave New World*.[42]

The charge has been leveled again and again that the Mayo group stands on the side of management and regards the industrial scene on the basis of an unquestioning acceptance of the goals of management. This bias is said to be evidenced by their concern with "cooperation" and "efficient running of the organization," and is all the more regrettable in view of their professed desire to bury all value considerations in the interest of "science." Perhaps the strongest statement regarding this charge is Sheppard's epithet, "managerial sociology."[43] Moore likewise speaks of the

> emphasis on the necessity of developing the "skills" of cooperation in industry, without reference to the aims of cooperative endeavor, the distribution of the product, or the distinct interest of the cooperators. Thus, Mayo's repeated comparison of the industrial researchers to the physician neglects the uncomfortable fact that in the former case the end to be pursued is not nearly so commonly agreed upon as in the latter.[44]

Koivisto charges that human relations studies are explicit in advocating cooperation, but that they fail to state that the goal of this cooperation is "to enable the organization to function efficiently."[45] In a reference to a comment from *Management and the Worker* he observes: "Here the idea of 'collaboration,' like the concepts of 'morale' and 'cooperation' is equated with management's idea of productive efficiency on the part of the worker."[46] Later he states: "The only objection that can be raised is that this evaluative context is implicit rather than explicitly stated."[47]

C. W. Mills raises the matter of bias in much the same way.

> What is the value content of these key terms (cooperation and collaboration)? It would seem offhand that, not questioning the managerial aim, the human relations experts

---

[42]*Loc. cit.*, p. 88.
[43]"The Treatment of Unions in 'Managerial Sociology,' " *loc. cit.*
[44]"Current Issues in Industrial Sociology," *loc. cit.*, p. 654.
[45]*Loc. cit.*, p. 565.　　　　　[47]*Ibid.*, p. 569.
[46]*Ibid.*, p. 567.

employ such terms in their effort to forward it: "...problems of absenteeism, labor turnover, 'wild-cat' strikes, show that we do not know how to ensure spontaneity of cooperation; that is, teamwork" (from Mayo). This assertion would seem to indicate that "we" in connection with "cooperation" means managers, and that "cooperation" in this literature means cooperation of workers for managerially approved ends.[48]

Schneider also charges Mayo and his collaborators with a "pro-managerial bias" and states: "The industrial sociologists are actually attempting to show 'hardheaded businessmen' their own interests."[49] He points out that an examination of their value premises, and a consideration of alternatives and their consequences would add a great deal to the stature of their work as social science. Pointing out that the "rules of the game" in labor-management relations are still far from being clear and definitely established, he argues that if industrial sociologists do no better than remain confined to their present orientation, "we may expect from them an unmitigated output of industrial cook-books written in a scientific vein.... Such an outcome might well be avoided by a determined attack upon the consequences of [alternative] value schemes."[50]

The Function of Collective Bargaining

Implicit in the majority of the criticisms cited in previous parts of this review, as well as explicit in some of them, is the charge that the facts and causes of a basic conflict of interest between workers and management have been overlooked. And because of this, attention has not been focused on the central problem area of industrial relations; namely, in what ways can this conflict best be accommodated?

This is the basis for the general criticism that the Mayo group has concerned itself only with superficial aspects of industrial relations. According to Sorenson, for instance: "Perhaps the most justifiably assailed characteristic of its approach [that of human relations in industry] is a rather exclusive concern with industry's vertical social structure and

[48]*Loc. cit.*, p. 210.   [50]*Ibid.*, p. 415.
[49]L. Schneider, *loc. cit.*, p. 414.

goals of social collaboration in preference to collective behavior *throughout* labor-management relations."[51]

Whereas Sorenson criticizes Mayo for overemphasizing the status aspect of industry, Bell directs a criticism at the persistent tendency to pose the problem of industrial harmony in terms of difficulties of communication:

> It is assumed that people don't understand each other because of emotional blocks or antiquated verbal habits, or because issues of feelings and status are involved....But industrial relations—like international relations—happen to be much less a problem of setting up a smoothly functioning organization than a problem of accommodating diverse and conflicting *interests*....The question of how to distribute increased income resulting from higher productivity, for example, cannot be flim-flammed away as a problem of verbal misinterpretation.[52]

The superficial analysis underlying the counseling program has been referred to scathingly in several articles. Schneider's reference to "a kind of limited psychiatric hearing for worker grievances" has been noted previously. Sheppard disagrees with the assumption that "any discontent among workers can be channeled into certain forms of activity which will not lead to disloyalty, hostility, absenteeism, restriction of output, and strikes, if they are persuaded to 'speak out' to someone."[53] Mills charges that the human relations group omits consideration "of the authoritative structure [of industry] and the degree of worker participation in it,"[54] and also thinks very little of a technique which allows employees "to 'blow off steam' without changing the structure of the worker's life in a sort of passive psychoanalytic relation which they would install in modern industry."[55]

The concepts of "status formations" and "informal organizations" (and the uses to which Mills says they would be put) do not fare much better in his evaluation than the counseling program:

[51]*Loc. cit.*, p. 263.   [52]*Loc. cit.*, p. 87–88.
[53]"The Social and Historical Philosophy of Elton Mayo," *loc. cit.* p. 399.
[54]*Loc. cit.*, p. 221.   [55]*Ibid.*

What have these students discovered other than (1) that within the authoritative structure of modern industry ["formal organizations"] there are status formations ["informal organizations"]; (2) that often these operate in resistance to the authorities and for the protection of the workers against the exercise of authority; (3) that therefore, for the sake of efficiency and to ward off uncollaborative tendencies [unions and worker solidarity], managers should not try to break up these formations, but rather to exploit them for their own ends...by recognizing and studying the status formations in order to manipulate the workers involved in them rather than merely authoritatively ordering them.[56]

Koivisto states:

Some studies seem to suggest that people should be happy with their places in the status system of industry, and devices such as interviewing can be used to increase their contentment. Golden and Ruttenberg, on the other hand, appear to feel that people in the work force are often not happy with their status, nor should they be. Rather the function of the union is to bring about greater economic equality and greater functional, social, and psychological equality.[57]

Koivisto also calls attention to the fact that writers outside the human relations school have emphasized different matters such as "union security, greater equality of income, and realistic collective bargaining."[58]

Dunlop has, perhaps, offered the most comprehensive criticism of the Mayo school's treatment of collective bargaining and has come closest to offering an alternative analytical framework. Much like the other critics, he paraphrases the Mayo approach: "The communication pattern or human relations between worker and foreman, foreman and steward, steward and worker, and similar relations throughout the organization constitute an explanation of the operations of unions and managements."[59] By way of contrast with the human relators' exclusive focus on interpersonal behavior, Dunlop distinguishes these types of industrial relations behavior:

[56]*Ibid.*
[57]*Loc. cit.*, p. 571.
[58]*Ibid.*
[59]*Loc. cit.*, p. 383.

(1) The *collective bargaining process*...The whole complex of interactions between the two organizations centering around the agreement and its administration is the behavior to be explained....

(2) The *management organization* [and] the *union organization*...Industrial relations behavior here is the separate activity of either organization.

(3) The *conduct of individual workers* in the work situation is the behavior to be explained.[60]

As he sees it, the human relations approach, while well adapted to the exploration of the third phenomenon, "is not the most fruitful framework" for the explanation of the first two types of industrial relations.

Dunlop, therefore, proposes a "larger framework"[61] which would take into account the fact noted by Blumer, that the accommodations between the two parties in industry is "between *organizations*," who have their own structure and life apart from the persons active within them at any given time. A further point emphasized by Dunlop is that "the accommodations between the two organizations takes place in *a particular environment*," with important implications which he spells out. His framework includes two further factors: first, "the *origins and beginnings* of a collective bargaining relationship," which he believes continue to be "an effective force" in their relations; and second, the particular *axes of development* which the parties come to select, and along which their relationship grows. This framework, says Dunlop, has the "advantage of concentrating attention upon the longer-run consequences of collective bargaining. The parties are not only affected by their environment, but as collective bargaining becomes more extensive, its processes also shape and mold the environment."[62]

Dunlop's view of what an analytical framework must include accounts, of course, for the deficiencies and errors he sees in "human relations" as a framework for analysis. He mentions the following: "The system of communications within a management or a union is in itself very largely a

[60]*Ibid.*, p. 384.   [62]*Ibid.*, p. 389.
[61]*Ibid.*, pp. 386–387.

product of other characteristics of the organization and its environment,"[63] and he adds, "An analytical framework . . . should make the influence of the context explicit rather than conceal it in the 'human relations' within organizations."[64] Dunlop asks: "What behavior of union or management organizations is explained by what variables?"[65] and he points out that scant attention has been paid to types (1) and (2) of industrial relations behavior (see above) in human relations studies. Commenting that the "interests and ideas regarding communications have been derived . . . largely from studies in which no union was present,"[66] Dunlop wonders how its conclusions can be carried over into the analysis of a collective bargaining situation where, he says, "Behavior in even the primary work community under union conditions is structured within narrow limits by the union and management organizations."[67] Next, Dunlop observes: "The communication and human relations approach seems to proceed from the premise that conflict can be reduced in industrial relations if individuals have more adequate information."[68] He contends: "The problems of conflict derive not from lack of knowledge or information, but rather from the difficulties of accommodating two organizations in a particular context."[69] His final criticism is a familiar one, and refers to the philosophic basis for the Mayo approach: "An analytical framework oriented toward the individual worker in his relationships to a single community of interests cannot provide a basis for a full explanation of the facts of collective bargaining."[70]

The Place of Unions

Some critics have voiced the suspicion that statements of Mayo and his colleagues suggest an actively antiunion attitude. But the general charge—and it is leveled by several critics, only some of whom seem to be ardent union partisans —is that the Mayo group, in both its theorizing and its

[63]*Ibid.*, p. 390. [67]*Ibid.*, p. 392.
[64]*Ibid.* [68]*Ibid.*
[65]*Ibid.*, p. 391. [69]*Ibid.*
[66]*Ibid.* [70]*Ibid.*, p. 393.

research, has made the serious mistake of ignoring unions. Thus, a leading character is missing from their drama of industrial· relations, and a major force in the life of the worker is left out.

Many critics have addressed themselves to the unfortunate results of this omission. Hart,[71] for one, believes that in overlooking unionism, Mayo failed to see one of the important remedies for the social isolation and moral confusion of the individual which is denoted by the word "anomie." He notes, too, that the omission has laid the group open to misrepresentation, in that their writings can be (and are) interpreted to mean that the reorganization of the worker and the industrial system can be achieved only by managerial action.

Moore asserts that "the emphasis upon the problems of management in directing the complex modern firm has obscured the role of the union in the organization of the enterprise and the interesting and scientifically significant questions relating to the union as a complex bureaucracy in its own right."[72] He then lists many problems of union organization and functioning which, although valid research topics, have so far been neglected. (He wrote in 1947.) He bemoans the fact that:

> The research situation almost appears to be one in which those whose primary concern is with the problems of management view the union as an uncomfortable external factor of significance only as it impinges upon the environment of managerial decision, while those interested in the "labor movement" hesitate to discuss any organizational fact that might seem less than favorable to the labor cause.[73]

Addressing himself to a different point, Blumer argues that the complexities of industrial relations simply cannot be studied and understood without attention to the labor organization as such. "Industrial relations are becoming increasingly a matter of alignment of organizations.... Unless the consideration of [the] front line of contact is made in the light of the relations between the organizations, the considera-

---

[71]*Loc. cit.*
[72]"Current Issues in Industrial Sociology," *loc. cit.*, p. 655.
[73]*Ibid.*

tion will give rise to only a deceptive portrayal of industrial relations."[74]

Ordway Tead, in his review of Mayo's *Social Problems of an Industrial Civilization*, notes Mayo's failure to realize the contributions made by unions to the very needs of workers which so concerned him. "There is...no full consideration of the role that may be played by labor unions in giving workers a total sense of security, self respect, and opportunity to voice complaints and suggestions."[75] He comments, "if this omission is intentional, it seems to me to represent a serious blind spot in thinking about and in analyzing this significant problem of employee participation and cooperation."[76] Mary Gilson[77] directed Mayo to find an answer to the question he posed in his preface to *Management and the Worker* (how can mankind's capacity for spontaneous cooperation be restored?) by reading Cook and Murray, *Organized Labor and Production,* a book which she regarded as having furnished the answer much better than the lengthy and elaborate Hawthorne research had done.

Mills is another critic who suggests that by overlooking unions, Mayo has failed to find possible answers to questions which concerned him:

> To borrow Mayo's language for a use to which he never puts it—unions in the last 20 years have secured the collaboration of at least one third of the U. S. wage and salary workers; surely this is an outstanding fact of cooperation in industrial life. But although these students are quite concerned with how effective loyalties are secured, they never study unions as centers for workers' loyalties....[78]

Mills charges the group with more than simple omission of unions. "When unions are not ignored, they are more likely to be taken as symptoms of trouble than as possible means of solving worthy problems."[79] And he comments: "There is little or no explicit mention of the class function of the union, nor its power function, but only of its status use."[80]

[74]*Loc. cit.*, p. 276.
[75]*Loc. cit.*, p. 180.
[76]*Ibid.*
[77]*Loc. cit.*

[78]*Loc. cit.*, p. 211.
[79]*Ibid.*, p. 212.
[80]*Ibid.*

According to Sheppard, too, a misunderstanding of the functions of unions is apparent. Commenting on remarks in Whitehead's *Leadership in a Free Society,* he states that Whitehead regards the "social" function of a union as corresponding to those of a social club: "In no way does it [the term social] include problems in classes, of distribution of political and economic power, conflicting ideologies."[81] In another article Sheppard specifically criticizes Mayo's concept of spontaneous collaboration, and attacks Mayo for promoting an idea which leaves out an important union function, since according to Mayo:

> cooperation in labor management affairs excludes formal contractual negotiations between the involved groups. In other words, spontaneous collaboration does not include collective bargaining: it does not mean union-management cooperation. The type of organization valued by spontaneous collaboration is vertical, not horizontal, which implies the company union.[82]

Conclusion

In conclusion, two points should be noted about these criticisms. The first is that, taken as a whole, they constitute as comprehensive an indictment of a theoretical system as could be imagined. Nothing more devastating could be said about such a system than that it is superficial and totally misses the point; that it originates in the personal bias of its creators rather than in the facts it seeks to explain; and that it is deliberately formulated to favor one social group over another.

The second point worthy of note is that these criticisms, however drastic they may be, in the main have not been directed at the school's empirical studies, but at those books which are expressions of the school's ideology. Chief among these are the writings of Mayo himself, in his *Human Problems of an Industrial Civilization, Social Problems of an*

[81]"The Treatment of Unionism in 'Managerial Sociology,'" *loc. cit.,* p. 311.
[82]"The Social and Historical Philosophy of Elton Mayo," *loc. cit.,* p. 398.

Industrial Civilization, and *Political Problems of an Industrial Civilization;* Whitehead's *Leadership in a Free Society;* and Roethlisberger's *Management and Morale. Management and the Worker*—the group's most empirical study, least suffused with ideology, dogma, and exhortation—has, however, suffered grievously from the poor reputation of these other writings because the critics have not explicitly sought to exclude this book from their attacks and at no time have dealt separately with it at length.

To prevent the book from being condemned with no better evidence against it than guilt by association, we propose to subject it to a critique confined initially to it alone. This implies that our defense of the book is not to be taken as a defense of the writings of the Mayo school as a whole. While critics of the school in turn have often been guilty of exaggeration and emotional bias, we tend to agree more than to disagree with them. On the other hand, the attempt to distinguish some aspects of *Management and the Worker* from other writings of the Mayo school is not an effort to duck the criticisms directed against the approach with which it is identified. The fact that *Management and the Worker* belongs to the genre is undeniable since Mayo's help and guidance is explicitly acknowledged in several places (e.g. footnote, p. 272). On the contrary, a great deal is to be learned from a joint consideration of *Management and the Worker* and the criticisms of the human relations approach. In order to accomplish this, however, it is necessary to distinguish between the criticisms which are largely relevant to those writings where ideology is prominent, and those points which are actually relevant to the empirical book, *Management and the Worker.*[83] The latter are obviously not unrelated to the former, but there are clear differences.

[83]One critic, C. W. Mills, does make several references to statements in *Management and the Worker* when arguing against the ideology of the human relations group. Most of these references, however, are confined to the section in which Mills takes particular issue with the counseling program at Hawthorne.

CHAPTER IV

The Hawthorne Studies:

Guilty as Charged?

ONE of the most important and yet one of the most easily overlooked points of difference between *Management and the Worker* and other products of the human relations school is in their tone of presentation. Kerr has suggested the tone of the latter by his remark that in their writings " are found the essential doctrines of the school."[1] *Management and the Worker* on the other hand, especially in the parts preceding Part V, is much more a book of data than of doctrine, and its tone differs correspondingly.

Mayo's work in particular has about it an air of omniscience and finality which, rightly or wrongly, has rubbed many a reader the wrong way. Definitiveness is bound to be felt as inappropriate when dealing with problems as manifestly complicated as industrial unrest. The very titles of Mayo's works suggest that a complete diagnosis of the ills of our society is now available for, after all, not much (except the economic!) remains after writing about the human, social, and political problems of our industrial civilization.

In contrast, *Management and the Worker* is neither written in a dogmatic style, nor does it— until the end—generalize

[1]Clark Kerr, "What Became of the Independent Spirit," *Fortune*, Vol. 48, 1953, p. 111.

much beyond the immediate findings. Even Mayo, in his preface to the book, points up its exploratory nature. After stating that "in the end a considerable enlightenment was gained," he continues: "In using the phrase 'considerable enlightenment' I must not be understood to claim that it was very extensive or very profound; the authors of this book and those who participated in the work would alike repudiate such a claim" (p. *xii*). The authors of the book likewise state at the very beginning (p. 4) that they decided to adopt a "narrative account of what was done step by step" although it "would bear the stamp of human imperfection." The flavor of most of the book is truly tentative, and the "weak places" have not been strengthened nor "the facade" made more imposing. As an example of this agreeable absence of dogmatism one may cite the discussion of what was, after all, one of the starting points of the whole inquiry: exploration of "the relation between conditions of work and the incidence of fatigue and monotony," to which Part I of the book is devoted.

It would be incorrect to say that scientific moderation is maintained throughout this part. The authors' statement, for example, that "the attitudes of the employee [i.e. neither lessened fatigue nor the wage incentive system] stood out as being of *predominant* importance" (italics added) represents their own evaluation of the results of these experiments rather than a fact which they were in a position to prove conclusively by objective means. Reference, too, is made to "stores of latent energy and productive cooperation which clearly could be obtained...under the right conditions."

Yet between the beginning of the Relay Assembly Test Room experiment at the beginning of Part I, and the interpretation of this and the two subsequent experiments at the end of Part I, the authors supply the reader with a host of data which allow him to make his own evaluation of the many interfering factors with which the study was bedevilled and which allow him to query the authors' conclusions. Indeed, some of the data on output and productivity rates warrants much closer scrutiny than has been given to it by most critics. Some of the increases in productivity which are said to have occurred actually are far from clear-cut. For example, in the case of the Relay Assembly Test Room, the average hourly output of some operators in the famous Period XII (original working conditions) declined exactly as one would expect it to on the basis of fatigue and monotony. The authors recognize this in part, for they state with respect to the monotony hypothesis that "no definite conclusion can be drawn" (p. 127).

It is, however, laudable that the authors at least present some data which point up the influence of monotony and fatigue, since it was the "fatigue and monotony hypothesis" which they were most anxious to disprove. In addition, the inability to have the girls work on exactly comparable relay assemblies; the need to replace two of the original operators in the Relay Assembly Test Room experiment with two, more cooperative (?) individuals; the effect of the slump; the unique position of these experimental groups; and the attitudes of supervisors to the experiments are all discussed and their possible effects weighed.

The point we wish to make is that not only data tending to support the authors' leanings are presented, but data contrary to it are also fully disclosed. The sections dealing with the Relay Assembly Test Room and subsequent ones on the Mica Splitting Test Room and on the Second Relay Assembly Group are excellent cautionary tales of the difficulties likely to be encountered by one who attempts to conduct and interpret research in industry no matter whether his research interests are in the orthodox field of industrial psychology, or in the newer social psychology of industry, or even in the economics of the individual firm. From this, the pedagogic point of view alone, the book is worthy of study.

This discussion of the difference between Mayo's rather dogmatic tone and the more open-minded approach of Roethlisberger and Dickson might well be concluded by drawing attention to some of the critics' own failings in this respect. For example, they have subjected the putative motivation and the level of professional integrity of the human relations researchers to a form of unfriendly public scrutiny which must be quite rare in the literature of the social sciences. The critics have also been exceedingly repetitious in the arguments they have used and have sometimes been guilty of factual errors and errors in interpretation which may have furthered their arguments, but which have certainly not materially aided scientific progress. Some of these errors will be mentioned in the following paragraphs.

The Question of Antiunion Bias

Management and the Worker, as well as other publications of the Harvard group, has been cited as guilty of withholding attention from unions. C. Wright Mills (in a statement which exaggerates the length of time the research at Hawthorne was pursued[2]) charges: "In a 15 year study of a giant industry, executed mainly during the Thirties, a decade when union membership increased approximately 250 percent, one finds no comment on unions."[3] Gilson, in her aforementioned review of *Management and the Worker,* states her belief that the counselors must have had some echoes of dissatisfaction due to the lack of recognition of unions when Western Electric paid more than $28,000[4] between 1933 and 1936 for espionage—and she wonders why the reader learns nothing of this.

[2]Other authors have mentioned shorter periods. Daniel Bell, on p. 81 of his previously cited article, "Adjusting Men to Machines," *Commentary,* Vol. 3, 1947, refers (admittedly ambiguously) to "more than nine years." Benjamin B. Selekman, who was associated with the researchers, names the five years between 1927–1932 as the field work period, in his "Discussion" following Mills' paper. See "The Role of Various Disciplines in Industrial Relations Research," *Proceedings of the First Annual Meeting,* Industrial Relations Research Association, Vol. I, 1948, p. 231.

[3]"The Contribution of Sociology to Studies of Industrial Relations," *ibid.,* p. 211.

[4]This figure is taken from the following: U. S. Congress, Senate, Committee on Education and Labor, *Report No. 46,* 75th Congress, 2nd Session. Washington: Government Printing Office, 1937, Part III, p. 88. Quoted by Mary B. Gilson in her "Review of Roethlisberger and Dickson, *Management and the Worker,"* American Journal of Sociology, Vol. 46, 1940, p. 101.

It would be disingenuous to attempt to see anything pro-union in *Management and the Worker*. However, there have been two statements defending the omission of unions in this research which seem to answer these criticisms. Hart, although writing an article deploring the lack of attention to unions on the part of "the Elton Mayo school," would set the record straight as to the time relation between the conduct of the Hawthorne research and union development in the country as a whole:

> The Hawthorne studies were made at a time when there were no unions in the Hawthorne plant of Western Electric, nor did unionism bulk so large on the American labor scene as it does now. The Hawthorne study was in the pre-CIO period, and there is no reason to believe that the worker at Hawthorne in '29 and '30 was any more union-conscious than the Roethlisberger and Dickson material shows him to have been.[5]

A similar statement has been made by Selekman, who was associated with the Hawthorne researchers. He contends that it is understandable that "very little articulation on trade union matters" appeared in the interviews with the workers. Although

> it is true that these studies were written and published in the 1930's, when trade unionism was spreading swiftly through American industry...it is also significantly true that the field work at the Hawthorne plant was carried on during the years 1927–1932...when trade unionism was at a very low ebb generally throughout the country. Nor did trade unions enter...the Western Electric Company...until the 1940's.[6]

But even if there had been no good reason for the omission of unions from the book, it would still be wrong to jump to the conclusion that it has a promanagement orientation. At least, *Management and the Worker* does not constitute a defense of managerial practices at the Hawthorne plant. On the contrary, the data presented in *Management and the*

[5]"Industrial Relations Research and Social Theory," *Canadian Journal of Economics and Political Science,* Vol. 15, 1949, p. 56.

[6]*Loc. cit.,* pp. 229–232, n. b. p. 232.

Worker, as well as the researchers' avowed purpose in conducting certain parts of this complex study, are such as to leave the reader with the impression that Western Electric was a thoroughly unpleasant place at which to work during those years and that the authors knew it. Nor is it likely that the authors could have been completely innocent of the fact that the reader would be left with such an impression. Occasional footnotes which warn the reader against the unrepresentative nature of the authors' selection of data, as well as citation of statements by workers which were favorable to the company, do not erase the impression left by the data in the body of the book itself. Their admitted obligation to the company makes their willingness to portray the situation accurately all the more impressive.

The conclusion drawn from the Relay Assembly Test Room experiment—namely, that the girls' release from oppressive supervision as exercised in their regular department was a chief determinant of their favorable response to the experiment—is but the first, albeit indirect, indication of what the true state of affairs at Hawthorne must have been during those years. The whole of Part II, which is an outgrowth of the Relay Assembly Test Room experiment and its related experiments, is based on the premise that operators have many complaints which should be heard and analyzed, and that the viewpoint implicit in these complaints should be impressed on supervisors.

There can be little doubt that the last chapter of Part II of the book contains much direct evidence of the unsatisfactory treatment of employees, evidence which, as we have said, was already implicit in the records of the Relay Assembly Test Room experiments. This chapter contains the statistical analysis of comments made on various topics during interviews and reveals, in the first instance, that almost half of the workers interviewed mentioned supervision spontaneously (p. 243). Next, analyzing the predominant "tone" with which supervisors were mentioned, the authors comment that while this "tone" comes out as "neutral" on the average, this result is due to many complaints being *balanced* by many favorable statements. It is not due to widespread, literal "neutrality." Moreover, the explanation for the variability in the reaction of workers to their supervisors is ascribed to differences in the behavior of different supervisors, and not to idiosyncratic variations in the reactions of workers to the same supervisor (p. 249).

Lest the interview program on which Parts II and III are based be taken to indicate a promanagement, "counseling-adjusting" bias, it should be emphasized again that the non-directive counseling program came much later and was separate altogether from the Hawthorne Studies as reported in *Management and the Worker*. The interviews reported on in Part II were conducted—let it be emphasized—more or less on a set question-and-answer basis. Even modifications introduced in Part III, which made the interview technique a more flexible one, had very little to do with the nondirective counseling system introduced in 1936, many years after the completion of these studies. The relief which workers obtained from being interviewed was at that time no more to the authors than one of "the most unexpected results of the program" (p. 227). The chief benefits of these early interviews were (1) an extensive effort to remedy evils so far as they pertained to physical plant conditions, safety, and health; and (2) the gathering of material for training supervisors.

Nor should it be thought that the analysis of complaints contained in Part II simply shifts the blame for conditions at Hawthorne from top management to the lowly group of foremen. We have already mentioned that Part III of the book, while devoted chiefly to the analysis of employee dissatisfactions, also contains two chapters devoted to attitudes within the supervisory organization. It is clear from the data summarized in these final chapters of Part III that the lower supervisors had, in turn, much to complain of in the treatment they received from those above them, particularly so far as favoritism and unfulfilled promises of promotion were

concerned.[7] The total impression left on the reader by Parts II
and III of the book is that many of those who worked at
Hawthorne thought of it as a semisweated beehive, with individuals at all levels—including lower and middle supervision
—transferred arbitrarily from job to job and department to
department. Favoritism was not infrequent and serious personal tragedies were often callously ignored. It might seem
as if this characterization of the Western Electric Company
is at variance with the authors' own original description of
the company as one with progressive personnel policies. The
latter characterization remains accurate enough if viewed
against the practices of other companies at that time. The
policies, however, were clearly not sufficiently progressive to
meet employees' needs for security and autonomy even
halfway.

Image of the Worker

Sentiments and Irrationality. The sympathy with which
working conditions at Hawthorne were treated by the authors
might by itself allow one to predict that they would not view
workers' complaints simply as the product of irrationality and
sentiment. Nevertheless, this point is raised here because the
linking of sentiments to worker discontent in human relations
studies has been criticized. As we have seen, critics charge that
too little attention has been paid by Mayo and his followers
to aspects of the industrial system which can be rationally
viewed as legitimate causes for workers' complaints. Consequently, critics are impatient with individualized psychological explanations and particularly with the concept of sentiments which they have interpreted to mean "irrational
reactions."

It should first be made quite clear that the terms irrationality and sentiment are explicitly not used interchangeably in

[7]The fact that poor treatment of subordinates is linked to the treatment
which supervisors themselves receive, and not only to their personality characteristics, was not formally handled as a research topic until several years
later. See Daniel Katz et al, *Supervision, Productivity and Morale in an Office
Situation* (Ann Arbor: University of Michigan, 1951).

Management and the Worker. The authors describe expressions of sentiments as "nonfacts." By this they mean that they are statements "involving terms which do not refer primarily to sensory experiences" (p. 258), e.g. sight and hearing, or that they are statements which "contain terms for which no physical or logical operations exist which can be agreed upon as defining them" (p. 259). The authors do not intend to imply anything derogatory when they use the word "sentiment." The term simply denotes, for example, a worker's feelings about such matters as the adequacy of a given wage, or his bitterness over the lack of considerateness on the part of a foreman who insists that he work overtime while his wife is sick at home, unable to look after herself.

In this part of the book the authors were intent chiefly on weaning management away from the idea that the manipulation of easily measurable physical conditions alone could dissipate workers' complaints. They seem quite genuinely concerned to broaden the perspectives of management by impressing on them that workers' "hopes and fears" and the ideas which they had about "fair play" were as important as their physical well-being. The authors state quite specifically that in the case of such complaints "not based on physical circumstances . . . no inference can be drawn about the illogicality or irrationality of employees in particular" (216). Admittedly the authors state that "daydreaming, revery, fantasy and preoccupation" frequently entered into the determination of complaints based on sentiment. But in the light of their previous and later disavowals, it would seem best to interpret this to mean that complaints based on offended sentiments are deeply felt—that they are reacted to with emotion rather than experienced as discomfort. The words "daydreaming," and so forth, seem to describe the state of being aggrieved and not the rationality or irrationality of the grievance itself.

The distinction between "nonfacts," on the one hand, and "the irrational," on the other, is surely a well-accepted one. It is based on the fact that the individual's aims and the things he desires, as well as his standard of what is right and proper, are, in part at least, on the level of ultimates without thereby becoming irrational. They are in a different universe of discourse altogether from the one in which the standards of logic or illogic are appropriate. Those two words are most at home in the realm of "if you want to have such and such, then this is what you should do," i.e. in the realm of means, and not in that of ends.

Economic Security vs. Status Striving. The foregoing is not in itself an answer to the charge against Roethlisberger and Dickson that they exaggerated the importance of such sentiments as the striving for status and prestige above the desire for power, control, and economic wealth. Mills[8] criticized the Mayo group for this distortion in emphasis.

While the book is decidedly open to attack on this score, a careful distinction must be made between the actual data it contains and the interpretation offered in its last section. The verbatim interview material, as well as the description of some of the separate experiments, indicate that the economic situation of the individual employee and of the plant as a whole is very vividly present in the minds of the employees. The authors once again seem to have taken no steps to expunge such data from their case material. In one instance, they themselves were well aware of how potent a factor economic security could be, for they admit that a whole year's data from the Mica Splitting Test Room experiment had to be discarded "because of the operators' anxieties over the uncertain future of the Mica Splitting job...which...completely overshadowed the experimentally introduced changes" (p. 153). These anxieties were caused by dismissals in the department from which the operators had been drawn, and by the effects of the "dreaded depression" on employment at Hawthorne.[9]

[8]*Loc. cit.*, especially pp. 213–214.

[9]There is, of course, a difference between being aware of something and recognizing its full implications in practice and theory. The fact that the authors cannot be exonerated of a failure to see the full implications of the interruption of the Mica Splitting Test Room experiment is discussed below in Chapter V.

The authors, for no apparent reason, fail to draw attention to the fact that the rapidly worsening depression in all probability had an important influence on the atmosphere in the Bank Wiring Observation Room, and critics have likewise failed to note this point.

Interviews such as that with Mrs. Brown (p. 293) and, by admission of the authors, the "daily conversation" of the workers among themselves (p. 531) were full of comments on the economic pressure under which Hawthorne workers found themselves. Moreover it was the authors' avowed aim in parts of the book (Chapters XII–XIV) to show how a combination of familial and economic circumstances could affect the sentiments of the individual worker. The book is in fact redolent of the poverty and oppression of the twenties and early thirties, and all but one of the bank wiremen in the Bank Wiring Observation Room were described as "in poor financial condition" (p. 531). Unlike the topic of unionism, therefore, on which the employees had little to say, the sufferings of economic deprivation figured largely in their minds; the authors present full documentation of this fact and are themselves well aware of it.

Nevertheless, the Hawthorne Studies are so written and interpreted as to emphasize, not the employee's personal situation outside the plant, economic or otherwise, but "the employee's existing social relations within the plant: the social organization of the group with which he worked and his position in that group" (p. 374). The authors state that the worker's reaction to physical events, wages, and hours of working can only be understood if one understands his status in the company's social organization, and the extent to which his position allows him to fulfill "the social demands he is making of his work" (p. 375). For example, the authors think that perhaps the worker may be extremely sensitive to physical plant conditions since they are the chief factors which separate the operators from the supervisory personnel; they define the worker's low status, and hence he is easily made aware of them, feels resentful, and reacts to them chiefly as a symbol. It is in this context that the authors portray the plant as a social organization, in the sense that it consists of various aggregates of individuals among whom there are well-recognized differences in prestige. The differences between shop and office workers, lower and higher supervisors, and men and women are mentioned specifically.

The reason why the relative prestige or "status" aspect of these divisions was so much singled out for attention by the authors is given in a brief reference much later in the book. Here is actually the key to a great deal of what the authors chose to emphasize and what they decided to play down. In the chapter in which the analysis of the Bank Wiring Observation Room is begun—when discussing the relationship between the worker and his job—Roethlisberger and Dickson state that "the relation between a worker and his job...is ordinarily discussed in such terms as fatigue, monotony, learning, education, aptitudes and so on."
However,

> these...will not be discussed here. Rather, attention will be confined to some neglected aspects of the relation [namely] the worker's social status in the company, [which] depends in large part upon his job.... A given job carries with it many related factors which have social significance. Wages, for example, vary with occupation, and these wage differentials frequently serve to reinforce occupational stratification. The results of the interviewing program showed very clearly that the worker was quite as much concerned with differentials...as with the absolute amount of his wages (p. 543).

The same point is already made in the Foreword of the book written by C. G. Stoll, an official of the Western Electric Company, when he says that

> previous studies had indicated that the human reactions of people engaged in productive work have a much more important effect on their morale and efficiency than had previously been realized. The investigations reported in this book were undertaken in the hope that the light which they would throw on this little-understood subject would be of

real value in improving our methods of dealing with employees (p. *vii*).

The key phrase in the author's own statement is "some neglected aspects." The authors should, and may well be, taken to task for so completely ignoring the fact that the power and ownership aspect is usually among "the terms" in which the relation of the worker to his job is "ordinarily discussed."[10] But this does not alter the fact that the prestige aspect had been among those previously neglected in the literature and that, like it or not, this aspect does play a role in the individual's feelings about his work. This being so, it should not be left unanalyzed and unelaborated. Much inconclusive debate could be avoided if the discussion of the prestige aspect of jobs, groups, wages, and the like was seen as an addition and not an alternative to the literature of industrial relations. It may be said in general that much of the book should be read as a series of discoveries of hitherto unknown or at least unrecorded and ignored facets of the thinking of people in industry. The authors' balance between topics reflects what their particular study has to offer which had not, to any large extent, been written of and noted before. It need not be taken—either by critics, or by the authors themselves —as representing the final weight to be attached to various approaches.

The description of "group life" in the Bank Wiring Observation Room should, perhaps, also be read in this same light of describing that which had previously gone unnoted. The authors' chief aim appears to be to convey the astonishment they themselves evidently felt when first realizing how elaborate the relationship among the workers, their work, and their supervisors had become, despite the fact that from the official point of view they were simply individuals working next to one another. The group was seen as being agreed not only on what was to be regarded as a reasonable day's work,

[10]It should, however, be noted that what the authors finally say is that "the point of view which has been expressed here is that noneconomic motives...as well as economic ones are fundamental in behavior and business" (p. 557).

but also on what were the appropriate mechanisms for enforcing the standard so agreed, on how to behave toward supervisors, on spare time activities, on the standing of the individuals within the group, and so forth.

Why Informal Groups Exist. We now approach what is probably the basic point of difference between the Mayo school and its critics. It can best be demonstrated by investigating the ways in which each answers this question: why do small, informally organized groups crystallize out of the larger aggregate of status groups?

Mayo's answer seems clear (and much exception has been taken to it): groups exist because "the industrial worker wants...first, a method of living in social relationship with other people"[11] and "happiness and such sense of personal security as may be found in subordination of an individual to a common purpose."[12]

Once again, however, it is extremely important to realize that the studies which make up *Management and the Worker*, unlike Mayo's writings, are not as a rule pitched at such a level of generality. They chiefly contain data and, moreover, data which can be interpreted in a sense opposite to Mayo's and even partially supporting the stand of his critics. The authors, insofar as they interpreted their own data, do in fact seem to take a stand at least as close to that of the critics as to that of Mayo.

According to *Management and the Worker* there is nothing instinctual, irrational, or inevitable about the formation of "groups" out of a collection of individuals. The data in the very first part of the book would contradict the instinctual position, for the individuals involved in the Mica Splitting Test Room showed little evidence of a change in their attitude toward one another. As the authors put it: "The Relay Assembly Test Room was a 'group' story; the Mica Splitting Test Room was a story of 'individuals'" (p. 156). They did not

[11]*The Human Problems of an Industrial Civilization* (New York: The Macmillan Co., 1933), p. 18.
[12]*The Political Problems of an Industrial Civilization* (Boston: Graduate School of Business Administration, Harvard University, 1947), p. 21.

share social activities outside work, nor did they pace each other with, and help each other at, work within the Test Room (pp. 155–156). The authors' explanation is quite simple. "Under individual piecework each job was self-sufficient—there was no need of working together." The formation of groups is therefore seen as in part at least conditional, secondary, and as instrumental to the satisfaction of individual needs, including the need for security of income. This does not, of course, preclude the reinforcement given to group life from what is sometimes referred to as "the need for affiliation."

This approach to groups as secondary becomes even more important in the authors' study of the Bank Wiring Observation Room. The authors saw the setting of this study as follows:

> The significant problem for investigation appeared to be that of specifying the factors which give rise to such informal organization. In attempting to answer this question, the external function of one group, bank wiremen, was examined. This function could be characterized as that of resisting change. Following this lead, the position of the Bank Wiring Observation Room group in relation to the total company structure was then examined. This analysis led to the general conclusion that the informal organization of the bank wiring group arose primarily from the position of that group in the total company structure and its consequent relations with other groups within the company (p. 548).

In the analysis to which they refer, the authors had pointed to the conflict between engineers and supervisors on the one hand, and workers on the other, as the cause of informal organization on the latters' part. The authors, therefore, were quite clear that it was in order better to resist the pressure exerted on them by the other two groups that the workers organized informally and in conflict with management.[13] We

[13]Homans, whose *Human Group* has, since its appearance in 1950, been taken as the epitome of the Mayo theory of groups, is equally explicit on the reactive nature of group behavior. He says that "the adaptation of the group to its environment is partly determined by the nature of the environment,"

shall now analyze in greater detail Roethlisberger and Dickson's treatment of the idea of conflict.

Anomie and the Causes of Industrial Conflict

Some Clarifications. The accusation that the Mayo school has failed to analyze properly the causes of industrial unrest has—as we have seen—been the most basic criticism leveled against it. To whatever school the critics have in their turn belonged, they have regarded the industrial scene as inadequately portrayed by the Harvard group. Neither proponents of a purely economic theory of conflict (who maintain that conflict is caused directly by differences over the appropriate division of the joint product of industry between wages and profits), nor the proponents of a socially embellished economic theory (who maintain that conflicts in industry are but aspects of a class conflict which is society-wide, but whose ultimate cause is once again economic), nor yet the proponents of the institutional theory of conflict (who maintain that much of industrial conflict can be traced to a power struggle between management and unions, both of which are heavily affected by internal politics), none of these has regarded the Mayo school with favor. All three believe that the source of conflict is located "outside" the plant; all three are consequently exasperated by the failure of the Mayo school to consider economic and institutional movements outside the particular plant which is being investigated.

No simple refutation of this, the central and most serious point in the critics' array, will be attempted. None is possible in the context of a re-review of *Management and the Worker* in view of the dated, unique, and therefore limited nature of the book. But at the outset it is important to make three distinctions: between the fact of conflict and the particular forms which it may take, between the description of conflict and an analysis of its causes, and between more proximate and

---

although Homans shows later "how this adaptation is also in part determined by the internal development of the group." See George C. Homans, *The Human Group* (New York: Harcourt, Brace and Co., 1950), p. 94.

more ultimate causes. The distinction between the fact of conflict and its form is important because it makes clear that the absence of organized labor-management conflict at Hawthorne does not imply, either for the reader of the book or for its authors, that a state of conflict did not exist. It implies only that this conflict did not exist in the form which has become the most notable one since then, that is between organized labor and management.[14] The Mayo school described conflict at Hawthorne in terms of tensions between informally organized groups. It is strange that the school's critics should have interpreted this analysis as theoretically at variance with an analysis of conflict as it takes place between formally organized groups. The two are not all contradictory —they are simply different forms of the same phenomenon.

At the same time it must be recognized that the authors committed a well-nigh incredible sin of omission by not recognizing in 1939 that the conditions which they had observed some eight years earlier were precisely the ones which accounted for the rise of formal unionism in the intervening years. Their own analysis would have been fully congruent with such a conclusion. The authors—by wittingly or unwittingly failing to recognize this and state it—have done the field of human relations in industry an amount of harm which, in retrospect, appears to be almost irreparable.

The Facts of Conflict. However, the facts of worker-management conflict at Hawthorne are in no way obscured merely because the form in which it was found there differed from that more current today. They are thoroughly examined by the authors in Chapters XXIII and XXIV of the book (the last chapter of Part IV and the first of Part V, respectively). These two chapters are among the most important in the book, and contain whatever conceptual and analytic scheme

[14]The transitory, and certainly conditional, nature of any one particular manifestation of industrial conflict was strongly emphasized several years ago in a book of readings on this topic. See Arthur Kornhauser, Robert Dubin, Arthur M. Ross, eds., *Industrial Conflict* (New York: McGraw-Hill Book Co., Inc., 1954), particularly pp. 12–14. That they stress unorganized, informal conflict is noteworthy because none of the three authors is famous for his appreciation of the "human relations approach."

the authors constructed to explain the data presented by them in the previous five hundred pages.

The thesis of these two explanatory chapters—and particularly of the earlier one, which stays closer to the data—is not simple. This is so partly because of the complexity of the data, partly because the facts and the authors' ideology (which begins to show through at this point) were at times difficult-to-reconcile neighbors. The authors address themselves, in the first of the two chapters, to the phenomenon of output control which they decline any longer (p. 537) to call "restriction." The authors go to some length in denying that this control resulted directly from worker hostility toward management, i.e. in the sense of workers conceiving it as a means of retaliating against management. They also deny that control of output could have been caused by workers' desire to protect their jobs or wage rates. Instead, they emphasize its function in maintaining the internal cohesion of the group, seeing it as primarily an "integrating mechanism" which enhanced the solidarity of the group.

This, however, is not the end but only the beginning of their analysis, which is then broadened to include the factory as a whole. The factory they view as being divided into five main groups (p. 542): managers, technologists, supervisors, shop workers, and office workers. The latter group, in this shop-floor analysis, is largely ignored except as prestige foils for the shop operatives. Emphasis is primarily on the shop operatives and on their relationship to technologists and supervisors. The activities of both supervisors and technologists are seen, of course, to be entirely controlled by management. It is at management's behest that these two groups become the source of continual "interference and constraint" to the worker. The technologists' ceaseless efforts to make the worker's job more effective for the organization by altering it is a source of chronic insecurity to the worker, as well as an unpleasant reminder to him of his inferior status and power (p. 546). The role of the disciplinarian which management thrusts upon the supervisor has a similar constraining effect on the worker (p. 547). These threats to the worker's status and security were seen as the immediate causes of worker-management conflict and of informal group organization at Hawthorne, and they are graphically described and clearly recognized as such in *Management and the Worker*, although the word conflict is but rarely used.

The authors' general conclusion is "that the informal organization of the bank wiring group resulted primarily from the position of that group in the total company structure and its consequent relations with other groups within the company" (p. 548), and that the chief function of the group was "that of resisting change" (p. 548). Plant-wide technological change, not the quality of face-to-face relationships, is their major explanatory variable. To resist such change, workers form groups; and to maintain such groups, mechanisms for the control of individual behavior—including output behavior—are created.

The authors quite specifically argue against the theory that this situation would be capable of improvement through mere changes in interpersonal relations at the first-line supervisory level. They state explicitly that supervisory training could not solve the problem (p. 537) since little can be done "by sheer force of personality" (p. 536). For years we have been accustomed to trace the rationale of supervisory training back to the "lessons" of the Hawthorne Studies. Yet the authors foreshadowed the failure of attempting to dispel conflict through improved face-to-face practices some seventeen years before actual studies of the effects of supervisory training caught up with them. The success of the experimenters' "supervision" in the Relay Assembly Test Room resulted from their power in holding at bay management's customary practice of changing job assignments, and the like. It did not result from the experimenters' "nice personalities." The significance of this distinction has never been adequately realized by either side in this controversy. In their study, therefore, the authors can most certainly not be accused of concentrating on the internal dynamics of the small group at the expense of analyzing its position in the organizational environment.

In the second of the two theoretical chapters, the authors' concepts are more clearly defined. The term "social system" is introduced, but it is defined in such a way that the concept carries with it no built-in bias toward a theory of nonconflicting interests. Instead, the words simply denote the fact that the authors visualize a factory as "something which must be considered as a whole, because each part bears a relation of inter-dependence to every other part" (p. 551). Thus "social system" refers to a formal quality, namely, that of cause-and-effect interdependence, and the fact that "any changes in one part of the social system are accompanied by changes in other parts of the system" (p. 567). The concept does not specify the content or mood of such interdependence—e.g. that it is necessarily cooperative interdependence.

In their use of other cognate terms—e.g. "the human [as distinct from the technical] organization of the plant"—the authors, however, are decidedly more ambiguous, for they refer here to the "collective purpose of the total organization" (p. 553). Moreover, it is here that we find the collaboration in the Relay Assembly Test Room defined as "higher" than that in the Bank Wiring Observation Room. This invidious comparison has irked many critics who have taken it as evidence that only collaboration which results in higher productivity specifically, and therefore is of help to management generally, is regarded by the authors as worth while. It is true that here in the first chapter of Part V are to be found the first signs of the "this-is-how-human-relations-can-help-management" orientation which comes out so strongly in the last two chapters. The emphasis, however, is still on the incompatibility of management ideology and innovation, and worker sentiments. While one instance of cooperation between the two sides is mentioned, the tone of the chapter is neither that of advice-giving nor that of optimistic prediction, but rather that of defining fairly clearly the lines of division. The authors can be given a clean bill of health even in their use of the term "higher" to describe the level of collaboration in the Relay Assembly Test Room. The authors did not use the term to denote collaboration helpful to management. Collaboration among the Relay Assembly Test Room workers was termed higher because that group was not so divided internally as were the bank wiremen, nor did the Test Room workers have to employ sanctions to obtain conformity to their norms. From that point of view alone, their cooperation can legitimately be described as higher and more spontaneous.

This description and analysis of the conflict situation at Hawthorne will probably surprise those who have assumed that Roethlisberger and Dickson's analysis would duplicate Mayo's, since Mayo put major emphasis on the social isolation and disorientation of the individual. It will also surprise those who would expect the authors to deal no further with conflict than to express their abhorrence of it[15] or who have seen the book as emphasizing primarily those factors in the work situation which unite workers and management.[16] Finally, the fact that the authors adopted this particular analysis of industrial conflict will surprise those who have equated human relations analyses with the description of mere errors in communication—an equation for which Homans justifiably rebuked Dunlop more than eight years ago.

The impression gained from reading summaries of the Bank Wiring Observation Room is that the book reaches its climax with the description of certain rather esoteric group behavior patterns, as those described in Chapter XXI. This impression corresponds with the facts only partially; at least as good a case can be made for selecting as the climax Chapter

[15]E.g. Bendix and Fisher, "The Perspectives of Elton Mayo," *Review of Economics and Statistics*, Vol. 31, No. 4, 1949, pp. 312–321. Also on this point, see Robert E. Sorenson, "The Concept of Conflict in Industrial Sociology," *Social Forces*, Vol. 29, No. 3, 1951, pp. 263–267.

[16]Cf. Robert C. Stone, "Conflicting Approaches to the Study of Worker-Management Relations," *Social Forces*, Vol. 31, 1952, pp. 117–124. It should be noted that Stone does not dismiss these "associative" factors as nonexistent. Rather he recommends that their study be supplemented by the study of dissociative forces along traditional, Marxist, conflict-of-interest lines.

XXIII, the final chapter of Part IV, in which the division between workers, technicians, supervisors, and managers is represented in quite unmistakable terms.

The Analysis of Basic Causes. If the authors may be acquitted, therefore, on the charge of ignoring the fact of conflict, what can be said of their analysis of its more ultimate causes? It is the failure to analyze adequately the more ultimate causes of industrial conflict, particularly the "extra-plant aggregation of economic and sociopolitical factors within which behavioral patterns and relationships...are structured,"[17] which in general has been most heavily emphasized by critics of the human relations approach.

That the authors are much more open to attack on this point can hardly be denied. On the level of theory, they have nothing to offer equivalent to the analysis of the economic determinist, who would swiftly refer management's restless pressure for technological improvement back to the nature of a competitive, private enterprise economy. In a market where competition is fierce, the pressure to reduce costs is inescapable, since total failure is the fate of whoever falls behind in the race. Hence, management must innovate.

The authors of *Management and the Worker,* however, have no such theory, or if they do, they do not state it. They pay but little attention to the coercive nature of the organization's economic environment. There is only one brief reference (describing the futility of workers' efforts to control piece rates through restriction of output) to the fact that "changes in piece rates, hours of work, number of people employed, and so on, frequently lie completely outside the control of the worker and *even of management*" (p. 534, italics added). Apart from this, the effect of the environment on management policies is not analyzed. No alternative theory as to why management should constantly drive technologists to innovate is put forth. Such questions as whether management controls the frequency of innovation and the rate at

[17]Abraham J. Siegel, "The Economic Environment in Human Relations Research," in Arensberg *et al.,* eds., *Research in Industrial Human Relations* (New York: Harper & Brothers, 1957), pp. 87–88.

which an innovation is introduced are not discussed by the authors.

The authors' analysis, therefore, ends at the brink. It does not deny the existence of conflict even though, because of the realities of the situation, the informally organized manifestations of conflict were described rather than its manifestations via unions and overt strikes. Nor, in their explanatory theory, do the authors attribute much importance to what might be termed mere "frictional" causes of conflict, such as insensitive supervisory behavior. The authors' major explanatory variable is constant technological change, and the disquieting effects of such change on occupational prestige groupings. Whatever "skills" may be demanded of management to avert conflict, they are definitely *not* merely interpersonal skills. After all, the authors specifically talk about management skills, not about supervisory skills, as being of crucial importance, and managers do not have face-to-face contact with working operatives. The only concrete example of the successful application of "managerial skill" contained in the book was of a group who were assured, and in the end almost convinced, that management really meant business when it promised not to introduce changes which would affect the stability of the group. No other specific examples were offered. The determining variable toward which their investigation had led was clearly not the kind which would respond to simple treatment. It had pushed the authors beyond the confines of the small group, and it would very likely lead them further—into a broader social investigation. Unfortunately, instead of following up the logic implicit in their analysis, the authors saw fit to add to the description of their empirical studies a set of recommendations to management in the form of the counseling program.

The Setting of the Study and Anomie. We are now in a position to understand why the concept of anomie—however important it might have been in the writings of Mayo—was of some, but only tangential, relevance to data contained in *Management and the Worker*. For better or for worse, *Man-*

agement and the Worker contains practically no social statistics on the work force of Hawthorne as a whole, which is a very serious omission. It is apparent from one of these statistical references,[18] however, and from the data presented about the individuals involved in the experiments and interviews, that the Hawthorne plant drew many of its workers from immigrants or second-generation Americans. Many of them were young, many were unmarried women, a high proportion were unskilled or semiskilled. Many of them had troubles at home, often based on parent-child differences in cultural allegiance and rules of behavior. Clearly this is not a group of workers likely to impress the outsider with their stable attachments to the local community (nor, for that matter, is it likely to be good material for unionization). If the concept of anomie is ever applicable, it is likely to apply to a rootless group such as this.

Mayo went on to generalize from the Chicago of the mid-twenties to industrial society everywhere, and does not seem to have considered that he might be dealing with a situation which was admittedly far from unique, but which was not necessarily a permanent characteristic of America as a whole. He was watching the bubbles of the melting pot, forgetting that a good alloy might appear in the end, even without the aid of a "plant society." Nor should it be forgotten by the critics that Marx too makes provisions for a group such as this in his concept of *lumpenproletariat*—a concept for which he has never been criticized, and certainly not by Mayo's critics. It seems that the name of a rose, and perhaps even its color, can after all make it a sweeter flower. Certainly Mayo is not alone in being a prophet of doom, nor is he alone in producing an unconvincing *deus ex machina* to eradicate the evils he describes.

Much more relevant to our argument than any possible error on Mayo's part is the fact that *Management and the*

[18]"In 1927...the company employed approximately 29,000 workers representing some 60 nationalities. About 75% of the employees were American born. The Poles and Czechoslovakians were by far the largest foreign groups. ..." (p. 6).

Worker itself contains little comment on the disorganization of society as a whole, nor on the role of the factory in stemming it. It is even possible that Mayo's vision of the factory as a substitute for the torn social bonds of the lost traditional society is derived, insofar as the Hawthorne material is concerned, from a mere two cases.[19] The two cases were Operator M1 in the Mica Splitting Test Room and Operator 2 in the Relay Assembly Test Room, who, after joining their respective groups, settled down well to their work for the first time in their careers. They had previously been looked upon as difficult personalities, and their maladjustment had been ascribed in part at least to their family circumstances. Whatever generalization Mayo may have based on these two cases, in *Management and the Worker* itself no more is said about them than that they seemed to indicate that "persons in human surroundings at work which suited and sustained them were able to carry a burden of domestic difficulties without becoming depressed" (p. 323). To admit the truth of this is a long way from ascribing all in-plant difficulties to social or personal problems outside the plant, and the authors specifically repudiate such an interpretation.

Nor does the above quotation imply that suitable work conditions would inevitably adjust the worker to his problem. On the contrary, in the one place where the authors do explicitly discuss the relationship between plant and community (p. 372), their tone implies that they regard it as thoroughly unhealthy for workers to regard the company as "father, mother, society and state all rolled up into one." Such a condition springs from "an impoverished social reality," is

[19]It might even be that Donham's notorious Foreword remarks—singled out for criticism by Hart *(loc. cit.)*, and by Kerr *(loc. cit.,* p. 134), who cites this excerpt: "industrial administrators have succeeded in making factory groups so stable in their attitudes of group cooperation that men in the groups explicitly recognize that the factory has become for them the stabilizing force around which they develop satisfying lives...in spite of...social chaos in the community outside"—were an interpretation by Donham of an interpretation by Mayo based partly on these two cases! Wallace B. Donham, Foreword to Mayo, *Social Problems of an Industrial Civilization* (Boston: Graduate School of Business Administration, Harvard University, 1945), p. *viii.*

a mere "compensation for lack of normal and adequate personal interrelations" and is likely to lead to an inability "to stand pressure of any kind. . . [to the making of] excessive and distorted demands. . . and to arouse sentiments of resistance." By way of contrast, "the more lines of loyalty extending outside the plant the supervisor has, the less urgent are his feelings of insecurity and the less excessive are the demands he projects on the company. Men with trades, foreign-born supervisors living in foreign settlements, and supervisors with active political or social affiliations seem, on the whole, more contented." This formulation of what constitutes a healthy, what an unhealthy, relationship between individual and plant would seem to coincide closely with the views of, for example, Kerr.

Lessons for Manipulators

The fifth and final part of *Management and the Worker* is entitled "Applications to Practice of Research Results," and its tone contrasts markedly with that of the preceding parts. The first of the three chapters in this part is, admittedly, innocuous and contains chiefly a summary of the authors' concept of the plant as a social organization. We might merely note that the authors take this opportunity at the end of the book to reiterate vigorously once again that informal organization and action in accord with "strong sentiments" exist at all levels of the organization—the managerial as well as that of the operators (p. 557).

The final two chapters, however, which are devoted in turn to the "Human Problems of Management" and to "Implications for Personnel Practice," are of a different kind. Both give the impression that they are "how-to-do-it" chapters: the one by not drawing a clear distinction between a rather generalized analysis of a problem and its solution; the other by giving details of the mechanics of an action program which, though initially described as diagnostic in purpose (p. 591), turns out later to be aimed at "adjustment" and "change" (p. 601).

The chapter on "Human Problems of Management" states that the functions of management are to secure the survival of the organization in the environment and to secure the cooperation of the individuals participating in the enterprise, a division made familiar by the earlier writings of Barnard[20] and by the more recent writings of Parsons.[21] It further describes the problems which are likely to arise in the course of fulfilling these functions. Nowhere do the authors claim explicitly that they can give instruction in how these problems are to be overcome. Yet there is an absence of the kind of reservation and disclaimers which marked earlier sections of the book, there is much ambiguous wording, and finally there is the reader's wish—and in all probability the authors' even stronger wish—that at the end of such a difficult road some substantial, practical benefit be forthcoming. All these elements conspire to give the impression that definite, concrete suggestions are being advanced. However strong the wish, the chapter on "Human Problems" in fact does no more than list the specific problems of management in some detail—those of technological and organizational change, of control and communication, and of the adjustment of the individual to the organization. The chapter is perhaps helpful in the sense that it points out—in connection with the problems of change—that the timing and method of introducing change are "very significant" (p. 579). Likewise, it advises management that the sentiments of people affected by change are "of prime importance." As for control and communication, it enjoins management to take care not to concentrate exclusively on transmitting information downwards, thereby overlooking the need to receive accurate communications from below. But however strong the initial impression, this chapter does not give management "the tools" for circumventing that resistance to change which the authors so dramatically described in their study of the bank wiremen.

[20]Chester I. Barnard, *The Functions of the Executive* (Boston: Harvard University Press, 1938).

[21]Talcott Parsons, "Sociological Approach to the Theory of Organization," *Administrative Science Quarterly*, Vol. 1, No. 2 (June 1956), pp. 63–85.

The contrast between the authors' misleading expansiveness in this last part of the book and the caution they showed earlier is perhaps best illustrated by their conclusion that

> the Relay Assembly Test Room experiment showed...that when innovations are introduced carefully and with regard to the actual sentiments of the workers, the workers are likely to develop a spontaneous type of informal organization which...is more likely to be in harmony with the aims of management (pp. 561–562).

Argyle[22] has pointed out, in connection with the Relay Assembly Test Room, that the authors had dealt with but *one* group in *one* particular setting, introducing *one* particular type of change. They were not in a position to say with certainty what caused the development of such an organization even in this one situation; they were certainly not in a position to draw far-reaching conclusions about management of the industrial scene in general. The implication that the supervisory techniques used in the Relay Assembly Test Room would have had similar results in the Bank Wiring Observation Room is particularly astonishing when one remembers that the authors themselves devoted several chapters to demonstrate and explain why the lessons of the original Relay Assembly Test Room could not be transferred even to a Second Relay Assembly Group.

If the first "how-to-do-it" chapter is deficient because its recommendations are too general, the second suffers because the very specificity of its recommendations make apparent their contradictory nature. It is this final chapter of the book which deals with the Hawthorne counseling program. This program grew out of the authors' unexpected discovery that talking about their problems left operators "feeling better." The program itself, however, was not begun until at least four years after the completion of the studies reported in *Management and the Worker,* and, except in this final chapter, there is no reference to it in the book. While the

---

[22]Michael Argyle, "The Relay Assembly Test Room in Retrospect," *Occupational Psychology,* Vol. 27, 1953, pp. 98–103.

mechanics of the program are briefly described, neither the reactions to it nor the results of it are presented. This too is in marked contrast to the reporting of the Hawthorne Studies proper. Yet this instrument, which the authors themselves describe as "still an experiment" (p. 604), is hastily advanced in these last pages as the authors' major contribution to research in, and practice of, personnel management.

The ambiguous nature of the program is apparent from the authors' description of it. The chapter both begins and ends with a definition of "the specific function of personnel work in industry" which emphasizes only the "adequate diagnosis and understanding of the actual human situations—both individual and group—within the factory" (p. 591). Moreover, throughout the description of the program, references abound to the "nonauthoritative" (pp. 596, 601) status of the counselor, and even to his refusal to give advice (p. 601). The manager alone, aware of all the facts including the nonhuman ones, is described as being in a position to act; the counselor seeks only to understand and relieve.

Yet, not only do the authors themselves state that this supposedly nonauthoritative "agency" serves to "control and direct those human processes which are not adequately controlled by the other agencies of management" (p. 601), but it is clear that this control comes, not via the incidental effects of interview-catharsis, but through the initiation of interviews which may perhaps be nondirective in form, but are anything but that in purpose and function. Apparently the counselor does not confine his activities to listening to the problems of individuals who approach him for assistance. On the contrary, counselors seem to initiate interviews with anyone, whether in the shops or in other parts of the organization, whenever their diagnosis of a problem leads them to think that it might be useful to do so. Not only the employee but the supervisor as well is, on the counselor's initiative,[23]

[23]A description and evaluation of the program confirms the impression that the counselor's role is more often an active than a passive one. See Jeanne L. and Harold L. Wilenski, "Personnel Counseling: The Hawthorne Case," *American Journal of Sociology*, Vol. 58, 1952, pp. 265–280.

"assisted" in directing his thinking "into those areas which he needs to take into account" (p. 602). This direction may include "certain aspects of the human situation which they might otherwise have overlooked" (p. 603). In this section of their description, the authors portray the counselor's role as being only secondarily that of a transmitter of information to management, and they put primary emphasis on the counselor's direct participation in the processes of individual adjustment, communication and control, and administering change.

The argument against nondirective counseling in a factory situation does not lie only in the ease with which it can be abused. To this the authors pay some, but not a great deal of attention. A counseling system is likely to have unfortunate repercussions, and one can draw this conclusion merely from the concepts developed by the authors themselves. The introduction of a body of counselors is, after all, a major change in the "social system" of a plant. Yet, remarkable as it may seem, the authors' analysis of this new role, and its relationship to the established line of authority, is made predominantly in terms of the technical requirements of production and in terms of the distribution of formal authority and functions! Not a word is said about the supervisor's threatened status (p. 596)! The authors recommend that authority be withheld from counselors because supervisors bear formal responsibility for production and hence must control all variables affecting it, and also because possession of authority would inhibit free communication between counselor and counselee. The authors seem to feel that their recommendation is enough to secure the success of the scheme. They do not seem to have anticipated that the mere presence of such an ill-defined and shadowy person as a counselor is likely to lead to insecurity and defensiveness on the part of many persons up and down the line. Yet, judging from the evaluation of the program which we have already cited, this confusingly powerful-powerless position of the counselor is a source of misunderstanding, guilt, and resentment, not only to many individuals at all

levels of the line organization but to the counselors themselves.

In short, the counseling program introduces new tensions,
and at best can be described as doing no more than to drain
such hostility as exists. Notwithstanding the genuine need
which such a program may well fill for some individuals
whose troubles are personal and not too severe, the counseling
program cannot in itself remove the causes of conflict, and
the authors' own earlier diagnosis ought to have made them
realize this.

The weakness of these recommendations makes it difficult
to understand why Friedmann should have praised (presumably with tongue in cheek) the authors for having "aided sig-
nificantly in the study and *reinforcement* of the means for
integrating the worker with the factory"[24] (italics added). The
reader's astonishment lessens when he realizes Friedmann's
error in attributing the establishment of the Hawthorne
Social Club to the Machiavellian designs of Roethlisberger
and Dickson. The authors' reference to these "integrative"
activities is in fact exceedingly brief (pp. 540–542), and the
activities themselves antedate the Hawthorne Studies by many
years.

Summary

We have now completed our re-examination of *Management and the Worker* conducted in the light of the criticisms
leveled against some or all of the Mayo school. Detail was
emphasized because at least some of these criticisms—if
intended specifically for *Management and the Worker*—turn
out to be based on errors of fact and of interpretation. This
chapter will have served its purpose if a sufficient number of
those who read it realize, perhaps for the first time, that (1)
the counseling program was a minor, and not a major, part
of the Hawthorne Studies; (2) that the authors explicitly
place no faith whatever in the efficacy of training supervisors

[24]Georges Friedmann, "The Philosophy Underlying the Hawthorne Investigations," *Social Forces*, Vol. 28, 1949, pp. 204–209.

in human relations skills; (3) that the authors explicitly state that managers as well as workers are moved by sentiments; (4) that neither group is thought of as irrational because they have sentiments; and (5) that the prime motive for the formation of the bank wiring group was the desire of the group to resist change, and not the desire to form a tribal society in miniature. It seemed worth while to correct these and the many other misconceptions about the book, because it has genuinely been a seminal work in the sense that much research has been inspired by it. Its arguments should therefore not be misunderstood; certainly it deserves far more attention in its own right than it has hitherto received. It is the purpose of this monograph to give it this long-deserved attention.

With the underbrush of such misconceptions as existed about the book cleared away, it remains for us to attempt to assess what general contribution the book has made to the development of human relations in industry specifically, and to those parts of the social sciences affected by it as a whole.

CHAPTER V

The Hawthorne Studies and the Development of Human Relations in Industry

ONLY twenty years have passed since the publication of the Hawthorne Studies which have always been regarded as the inaugural step in the creation of the field of human relations in industry. Such a brief timespan is inadequate for any final assessment of the studies and their influence. It is certainly inadequate for a final assessment of the entire field. Nevertheless, developments in the field have been such, particularly during the last few years, that at least a brief retrospective look extending back to the Hawthorne Studies and their lessons is of considerable interest.

This final chapter is devoted to the more general task of looking back. In the course of it, we shall try (1) to describe and explain the characteristics of the book as it stands, including within this rubric an explanation of the contradictions within the book to which we have already drawn some attention; (2) to describe and explain the more or less immediate impact which these studies had, including the reception given to them; and (3) to link the Hawthorne Studies to some of the recent developments in the field of human relations in industry.

Some Problems in Defining the Human Relations Approach

It will be noted that our approach to the field is deliberately a developmental, historical one, and not a definitive, dogmatic one. Before embarking on the task of assessment, it may be appropriate to point out briefly why the definitive approach to a delimitation of this field is not considered fruitful. This is not to say that there may not have been at one time a good deal of truth in some of the critical definitions which have been proposed, e.g. "plant sociology"[1]; nor is it intended to deny that some of those working in the field have maintained a uniform approach throughout the entire period; nor is our developmental approach to the field of human relations intended to deny that these critical definitions may have had a salutary effect on research.

Indeed, just because these definitions (and the accusations which they were intended to convey) have in part been effective in changing the field, the process of tracing the change is more enlightening than the presentation of a single "still picture" out of a sequence which is still changing in discernible directions. Any hard and fast drawing of boundaries around a hypothesized approach is, on the face of it, unlikely to remain accurate with an approach as new as this. It is even less likely to be accurate when done in the heat of battle and when the newcomer quite patently cuts across traditional disciplinary lines, so that our customary categories of thought cannot easily grapple with it. In fact, as a few early and friendly critics of the Hawthorne Studies pointed out, one of the major contributions of the book was its unorthodox approach.[2] There is, admittedly, a difference between an interdisciplinary approach and a totally undisciplined one! But while the book can at times be accused of the latter as well as praised for the former, its merits on the former, and many other related scores, are considerable.

[1] Bendix and Fisher, "The Perspectives of Elton Mayo," *Review of Economics and Statistics,* Vol. 31, 1949, pp. 312–321.

[2] E.g., C. W. M. Hart, "The Hawthorne Experiment," *Canadian Journal of Economics and Political Science,* Vol. 9, 1943, pp. 150–163; also V. W. Bladen, "Economics and Human Relations," *ibid.,* Vol. 14, 1948, pp. 301–311.

The unqualified equation of the human relations in industry approach with "plant sociology" is one example of a rather fruitless kind of academic gerrymandering. Such a definition can only be justified if Warner's *The Social System of the Modern Factory*[3] is excluded from the field. Since Warner with his anthropological background and his activities as a consultant to the Hawthorne experiments (p. 389) is invariably regarded as one of the founders of the school,[4] to exclude his writings hardly makes sense. Nevertheless, excluded they are, for while the titles of Warner's books are frequently listed in footnotes which purport to give typical examples of the writings of the human relations school, there is often no reference to their content. It has certainly never yet been pointed out that the Yankee City series of books (of which *The Social System of the Modern Factory* is the fourth volume) was *quite explicitly designed to begin where the Hawthorne Studies left off,* namely, with a study of the community—and broader, nationwide changes in social and economic structure.[5] Since this was the purpose of the Yankee City studies, it is not surprising that Warner's analysis of the Newburyport strike employs variables which would be acceptable to the most exacting "environmentalist." Warner did, admittedly, see the loss of status of the skilled workers within the plant as one of the contributing causes of the strike. But whereas the authors of *Management and the Worker* would have stopped at this point, Warner goes on to track down the ultimate causes of this and other changes. He finds them in the rapid geographic expansion of the market for the product concerned which, together with the invention of machinery, led to an increase in the optimum size of the firm. This in turn led to the elimination of the local elite from ownership and

[3]W. Lloyd Warner and J. O. Low, *The Social System of the Modern Factory* (New Haven: Yale University Press, 1941).

[4]See, e.g., O. Kerr and L. Fisher, "Plant Sociology: The Elite and the Aborigines," in *Common Frontiers of the Social Sciences* (Glencoe, Ill.: The Free Press, 1957), pp. 281–308.

[5]Warner makes this quite plain on p. 1 of his book and even here it has not been remarked by critics. W. Lloyd Warner and P. S. Lunt, *The Social Life of a Modern Community* (New Haven: Yale University Press, 1941).

management of the plant and to their replacement by financial remote control from outside the community. The lengthening of the bureaucratic hierarchy, which was a consequence of the increasing size of the firm and of a more complicated technology, is also noted, as are increasing restrictions on the social mobility of workers. Warner sees all these factors quite clearly as inherent in the industrial system as presently constituted, and not as peculiar to the plant studied. Very little attention is paid to interpersonal skills—or their absence— as possible causes of the Yankee City strike. Yet the thesis of this book is not once discussed by those who speak of "the" human relations school and of its neglect of the environment of the factory.

The imputation of other characteristics which are supposedly unique to, and definitive of the school, turn out to be equally dubious on closer examination. For example, equating human relations in industry with an almost exclusive reliance on unstructured interviewing and observation is no longer warranted. While Moore's attack on the field because of its use of these two "primitive methods"[6] may have been appropriate at the time it was made, it is now passé. Moore realized that his criticisms never applied to the Hawthorne experiments themselves, which—as was shown in Chapter II above—contain careful examinations of output figures and elaborate statistical analyses of interviews. (The latter may well be one of the earliest uses in an industrial setting of what has since become known as content analysis.) If the field were indeed characterized by the use of unstructured research techniques, plausible defenses of their employment could and have been made.[7] Certainly Schneider's assertion[8]—on a purely a priori basis—that in industry these

[6]Wilbert E. Moore, "Current Issues in Industrial Sociology," *American Sociological Review*, Vol. 12, 1947, p. 563.

[7]See G. C. Homans, "The Strategy of Industrial Sociology," *American Journal of Sociology*, Vol. 54, 1949, pp. 330–337; B. B. Gardner and William F. Whyte, "Methods for the Study of Human Relations in Industry," *American Sociological Review*, Vol. 11, 1946, pp. 509–515.

[8]E. V. Schneider, "Limitations on Observation," *Social Forces*, Vol. 28, 1950, pp. 279–284.

methods cannot yield reliable results because informants will be sure to conceal deviant behavior is disproved by every study from *Management and the Worker* onward.

The main point to be made in answer to Moore's attack— or definition—on methodological grounds is, however, that it is no longer appropriate. The Michigan studies of supervision—a very large group of studies to which we shall refer again in this chapter[9]—are highly quantitative and are at least partly based on testable prior hypotheses while at the same time being very definitely "plant sociology." Studies of unions have likewise been made using both quantitative and nonquantitative methods.[10] The existence of the latter studies proves also that unions have by no means been permanently neglected in this literature as is sometimes stated or implied. Some of the attempted definitions of the field clearly can only be justified if the definition is, in fact, used as a principle of selection—in which case it becomes tautologous.

The Michigan studies of supervision in industry pose another astonishing anomaly in this matter of the delimitation of the field of human relations in industry. These studies are never included in attacks on the field, yet it was their aim, more explicitly than in any of the studies usually criticized, "to discover the underlying principles applicable to the problems of organizing and *managing* human activity" and "to discover how to train persons to understand and *skillfully use* these principles."[11] These studies, much more than any of the so-called typical human relations studies, have focused exclusively on psychological variables pertinent to the small group and its immediate leadership. Only the failure to find the

For example, Nancy Morse, *Satisfactions in the White Collar Job,* (Ann Arbor: University of Michigan, 1953).

[10]For a quantitative study, see Lois R. Dean, "Union Activity and Dual Loyalty," *Industrial and Labor Relations Review,* Vol. 7, 1954, pp. 526–536. For a preponderantly nonquantitative study, see Leonard R. Sayles and George Strauss, *The Local Union: Its Place in the Industrial Plant* (New York: Harper & Brothers, 1953).

[11]Daniel Katz, Nathan Maccoby, and Nancy C. Morse, *Productivity, Supervision and Morale in an Office Situation* (Ann Arbor: University of Michigan, 1951). Italics added.

results hoped for forced those conducting the studies back, step by step, into the larger organizational environment.[12] Equally astonishing is the freedom from attack enjoyed so far by the followers of Lewin and the group-dynamics approach. Coch and French's action research: "Overcoming Resistance to Change"[13] is far more blatant in accepting management's goal of efficiency, and the desirability of manipulating workers to achieve it than any study ever undertaken by a follower of the late Elton Mayo.

The immunity enjoyed by the Michigan studies and the group dynamicians may result from the restricted reading of the critics (who are generally economists or those sociologists who are farthest removed from the area of social psychology). It may also be related to the more respectable academic parentage of these immune studies as compared with those conducted by a business school. In any case, there is some justification for saying that many of the characteristics regarded as unique to the Mayo school (such as the concentration on psychological variables and on small groups, and a preoccupation with manipulation) are much more clearly present in the writings of authors who had had no personal association with the Harvard group than to the Harvard group itself. We have already indicated that other purported hallmarks of the Harvard group, such as their neglect of structural changes in the economy, are in fact not uniformly characteristic of their writings at all.

Hence our conviction that in this still rapidly developing area of study, a historical approach to its definition and delimitation is more fruitful than one which seeks to trace boundaries and impute characteristics regardless of time.

[12]See, for example, Donald Pelz, "Influence: A Key to Effective Leadership in the First Line Supervisor," *Personnel,* Vol. 29, 1952, pp. 209–217.
[13]Lester Coch and John R. P. French, Jr., "Overcoming Resistance to Change," *Human Relations,* Vol. 1, 1948, pp. 512–532. More recently these and other group dynamic studies *have* been attacked, e.g. by William H. Whyte, *The Organization Man* (New York: Simon and Schuster, 1956).

Reception and Timing: The Discovery of Workers' Resistance to Change

The previous chapter was entitled "The Hawthorne Studies: Guilty as Charged?" and the separate sections into which it was divided sometimes ended with a "guilty," sometimes with a "not guilty." This is but one indication that *Management and the Worker* is a work of many aspects with different implications for different disciplines.

The best example of this is the authors' discovery, at the end of their studies, that groups of men organize to resist change. To those approaching the Hawthorne Studies with a background in labor history, this "discovery" comes as very much of an anticlimax. The best that we were able to say in defense of it (see above, Chapter IV, p. 63, the section titled *Anomie and the Causes of Industrial Conflict*) was that it showed the authors to be in agreement with others who have worked a long time in the field. We could not value their analysis for its novelty.

This puzzling lack of novelty becomes considerably more understandable when one remembers the setting of the book and its starting point. The Hawthorne Studies began as an investigation by industrial psychologists into the effects of physical working conditions on output. At the time when the studies were conducted, large segments of industrial psychology were oriented in what might be termed a radically behavioristic direction. Excluding all individual motivational factors (let alone social influences on the individual), these psychologists were conducting their research as if one could assume, for all practical purposes, that there exists a direct link between external environmental conditions (such as intensity of light, length of rest pauses) and behavioral end results (such as output). Likewise, some economists were still working with theories based on the assumption that individuals—including workers—planned their economic lives without reference to others and were motivated only by relatively short-term economic interests (Mayo's "rabble hypothesis").

Seen against this background, the significance of the authors' conclusions is not that they demonstrated to students of industrial relations that they were being insufficiently sociological and psychological, but instead, one must see the authors as demonstrating to industrial psychologists like themselves (as well as to noninstitutional economists) that industrial relations factors could not be ignored even in the heartland of industrial psychology: in the investigation of reactions to lighting and rest pauses. Though the authors fail to draw attention to this fact at the conclusion of their studies, there is no doubt that their findings should be read with this point in mind. The investigation of workers' reactions to variables typically reserved for research by industrial psychologists was, we repeat, the initial focus of the Hawthorne Studies, and the results of the studies are pertinent, in the first instance, to that focus.

It is not surprising, therefore, that the influence of the book upon industrial psychologists and their writings has turned out to be much more profound than its effect on the developing field of collective bargaining. Even a cursory glance at recently published texts in the field of industrial psychology will bear this out.[14] Increasingly, such texts have emphasized motivation, leadership, attitudes and the importance of group influences at the expense of practically all the traditional areas of industrial psychology with the exception of testing and selection.

It would, of course, be wrong to attribute this decline of interest in the traditional problems of industrial psychology to the Hawthorne Studies alone, for it is probably related also to the gradual improvement in hours and working conditions in the years after World War I. Once hours are reduced to a reasonable level, further cuts will not result in higher production, even if previous reductions from a much higher

[14]See, for example, Morris Viteles, *Motivation and Morale in Industry* (New York: W. W. Norton & Co., Inc., 1953); and Thomas A. Ryan, and Patricia C. Smith, *Principles of Industrial Psychology* (New York: Ronald Press Co., 1954); not to mention such deliberate modernists as Milton L. Blum in *Industrial Psychology and its Social Foundations* (New York: Harper & Brothers, 1949).

work load did have that effect. Under these new circumstances, motivation will genuinely rise in importance as a causal variable in industrial behavior, and factors such as physical fatigue will decline in importance. It is to this change in social conditions that at least part of the growing interest in human relations in industry, and of the declining interest in traditional industrial psychology, can be attributed. Changes in managerial ideology, as recently portrayed by Bendix,[15] played a further role in this change of emphasis, both in textbooks and in the industrial world to which the books are ultimately addressed.

It may be asked why so many critics failed to see the book in its original, chosen context. The answer lies in the timing of the book's publication. The book's timing explains far more than why the authors obtained no interview material on workers' attitudes to unions. The lessons in industrial relations which it contained were chiefly directed at industrial psychologists. They were meaningful and substantial enough in the superficially tranquil 1920's; and in their own original context they still remain so valid that industrial psychology has changed its character once and for all. But when it finally appeared, the book's lessons were judged in a completely different context from that of industrial psychology. By the late 1930's the industrial scene had changed completely, and readers—most particularly readers in the academic world—were far too aroused over what implications these changes might have for their own disciplines to assess carefully what specific question the book had been designed to answer.

By the late 1930's and the early 1940's many, with Blumer, felt strongly that the time was more than ripe for the behavioral sciences in general and for sociology in particular to tackle the problems posed by the new industrial relations. The field of industrial relations had so far been cultivated only by relatively small groups of social historians and economists, and was almost completely untilled so far as sociology

[15]Reinhard Bendix, *Work and Authority in Industry: Ideologies of Management in the Course of Industrialization* (New York: John Wiley and Sons, 1956).

was concerned. Sociologists had made no recent, useful contribution to it, and they were on the lookout for a book that would establish their claims. This need was not, and could not be satisfied by *Management and the Worker*. Sociologists, if not social psychologists, were looking for an analysis at the institutional level and at the level of social structure. The Hawthorne Studies, at least as much by virtue of the questions which they sought to answer as from any bias of their authors, ignored such an analysis or at best, could be said to take it for granted. The book can be used fruitfully to show what the implications of such an institutional analysis are for the analysis of individual and small group behavior in industry. Alternatively, one might say that the book contains the psychological underpinnings of an institutional analysis, whether sociological or economic. But in the absence of an existing, and sufficiently recent, socio-economic analysis at the institutional level itself, many sociologists in the late 1930's feared (not without some justification) that the book would be taken by everyone as a signpost along the road down which the behavioral sciences would henceforth seek to make their main contribution to the field of industrial relations. Most sociologists at that time were not prepared to follow this road, and since that time they have not shown any signs whatever of changing their minds.

It is, however, unfortunate that disappointment over the book's not meeting the grand requirements of the times, should have led so many critics into errors in interpreting the book, both as to its general import and as to its details. Viewed in the context in which we have sought to place it, the book's contribution is, we believe, profound and quite unrivaled. Nowhere will the researcher who delves into the more microscopic social phenomena find a better illustration and explanation of how even his data are deeply affected by certain "larger" variables, such as the nature of economic institutions, the state of technology, urban integration, ethnic feelings, size of organization, and so forth and so on.

Management and the Worker possesses many other merits,

however, quite apart from its lesson to industrial psychology. To these we shall now turn, taking up first its methodological contribution.

Problems for Theory in an Applied Field

The Book's Eclecticism. If the timing of the book was unfortunate because the very questions which it had posed at the beginning were passé or had paled in relative importance by the time the answers were available, so also was the book unfortunate because its methodological structure was out of tune with developments in both psychology and sociology during the 1930's. Not only was the book eclectic in the matter of research methods in the narrow sense (using at various times unstructured depth interviews, observation, content analysis, and documentary records—and none of them with the expert's élan), but it was also eclectic in its coverage of subject-matter areas. In fact, the feeling that the contribution of the Hawthorne Studies to the field of industrial relations is merely that of elaboration, and is in that sense marginal, recurs whenever the book is scrutinized from the vantage point of any particular specialty in social science theory.

The book is, despite its frequent use of quantitative data, not what would now be called a rigorous study. The authors do not posit a relationship between two or more variables, draw up a study-design and instruments to measure them, and measure the relationship which actually exists. Instead, they cover all the data and areas of investigation which their judgment told them were of relevance if they were to understand why the people they observed behaved in the way they did. This is, of course, somewhat similar to the descriptive case-study approach which was already growing unpopular in the 1930's. In sociology, just as in clinical psychology, the case study relies on the intensive and—as far as the number of variables are concerned—extensive investigation of a single unit, whether the unit is an individual, a group, an organization, or a society. Hence chapters dealing with the effect on work performance of the acculturation of ethnic Americans living in a large city in times of economic depression are followed by others dealing with the internal dynamics of a small group, and by still others which focus on occupational prestige patterns and the instability of these patterns in the face of technological change. The shortcomings are obvious enough of such a hit-and-run approach toward discrete academic areas of theoretical interest, each of which could profit from, and each of which is now customarily dealt with by, separate intensive investigations. It is not unlikely that some of the neglect which the book has suffered can be attributed to its lack of academic specialization. Its eclecticism makes the book genuinely difficult to fit into any one of those many specialties into which sociology and psychology have so rapidly been divided in the course of their phenomenal growth in the last twenty years.

Comprehensive and Abstractive Approaches to an Applied Field. Yet the book, and other contributions to the fields of industrial sociology and industrial social psychology shares these problems of "awkwardness of fit" with contributions to other concrete areas of social inquiry such as those of delinquency and of race relations. These fields gain their identity from the fact that they are important social problem areas, and not from any simple relationship to a single area of academic specialization and theory. Admittedly, some contributions to social problem areas *are* made from the vantage point of a single theoretical orientation, and with much good reason. These contributions are in line with a piecemeal, analytically abstract approach which may well be unavoidable if theoretical understanding of as well as practical aid to these areas is to advance. But such a specialized approach does suffer from being incomplete and to that extent misleading and removed from its field. It is so clearly not the whole story. The economic interpretation of racial discrimination fails to take note of the psycho-dynamic element which mobilizes feelings of prejudice in so many individuals; the group-membership theory of prejudice cannot account completely for changes in discriminatory behavior attendant upon a change in the law.

Hence in all those areas of investigation in which we are interested for the sake of their social significance and not alone for their use in building better theory, there will remain a niche for books which attempt to give a total picture. There will always be a desire to be shown how each of the separate theories operates in real life and how its predicted consequences modify and are modified by the operation of other theories culled from other academic specialties. Thus each specialist is not only helped to retain a sense of balance and realism, but by occasional immersion in the situation as it actually exists, he is also helped to gather fresh ideas. In these practically important fields, therefore, the growth of knowledge is likely to be, and is optimally, a dialectic one. Studies are likely to swing back and forth between rich but analytically limited and superficial description on the one hand, and rigorous but limited abstraction on the other. Any given contribution may of course contain both elements, but it is likely to lean toward one side or the other. In any case, we propose this dichotomy more as a perspective from which to view the process of growth of knowledge in these fields, than as a system for classifying research studies. Viewed from this perspective, the Hawthorne Studies gain their importance from the fact that they were comprehensive and encompassed a wide range of empirical data. They contained a rich description of an industrial situation at a time when the new fields of industrial sociology and industrial social psychology were at least as short on data about specific situations as they were on theory or theories. As a result, the Hawthorne Studies can be used to put into perspective any of the many theories which converge on these fields. Further, they can be used, and have been used, to crystallize new areas for theoretical investigation.

The Psychological Bias of the Comprehensive Approach. One further point should be made about the nature of comprehensive studies before we go on to demonstrate how *Management and the Worker* has been used, and could have been used even more, to stimulate new theoretical formulations and research. It is, of course, at the level of the individual that the manifold forces determining social action are ultimately summed up and balanced against one another. It should therefore come as no surprise that the type of study which we have called comprehensive inevitably tends to have something of a psychological bias. By this we mean that these studies tend to belong to that distinct and distinguished line of sociological writings which, like *The Polish Peasant*,[16] stress the individual's "definition of the situation" at the expense of pursuing the social-structural determinants of a single aspect of that situation.

However controversial such an approach and however irritating to those in particular who would like to see a clearly drawn boundary between sociology and psychology, the importance of understanding the psychological context in which any variable operates on the individual cannot be denied. To illustrate this importance we may cite the case of Marx, since his failure to take psychological variables into account is at least one of the reasons why his predictions turned out to be erroneous. Yet this is often forgotten by critics of *Management and the Worker* who accuse the book of being overly psychological, and who prefer a rather ill-defined sociological level of analysis.

Marx—like Veblen[17]—began at the societal, institutional level, analyzing systems of property ownership and of social classes based on such ownership. Both writers were concerned about predicting the future relationship between these objectively defined classes. The psychologically inclined critic cannot, of course, maintain that predictions which rely heavily upon institutional analysis are erroneous in principle, and certainly we would not wish to maintain such a stand. On the contrary, few analysts since Marx' time would think of using a theoretical schema which did not give some prominence to technological and institutional-economic variables. Indeed, the failure of Marx' predictions—as regards increasing misery

[16]W. I. Thomas and Florian Znaniecki, *The Polish Peasant in Europe and America* (Boston: R. G. Badger, 1918–1920).

[17]For a similar interpretation, see Bernard Rosenberg, *The Values of Veblen: A Critical Appraisal* (Washington: Public Affairs Press), pp. 87 et. seq.

and revolution—can be attributed partly to errors at his own level of objective analysis. Apart from his underestimation of the power of the democratic state as an independent force restraining the free play of economic forces, his chief error lay in his failure to foresee such objective changes as the growth of technical and therefore occupational diversification.

But even had he been able to forecast such specialization and other equally objective developments, Marx—had he wanted to predict their effect on the state of mind of the working and middle classes, and hence their effect on class warfare —would have required assumptions about motives, values, "sentiment," or what have you, which he could not articulate because they were outside his theoretical schema. What can be maintained by the psychologically inclined critic, therefore, is that predictions based on objectively defined variables alone have not been and cannot be successful.

Emphasis on the individual's definition of the situation need not in any case altogether preclude learning more about its objective aspects. On the contrary, a great deal is bound to be learned about the objective situation through psychologically oriented studies, simply because the nature of the situation must influence heavily what the individual informant perceives—and he often is consciously aware of this and reports it. Moreover, like Warner, many of those investigating the individual's perception of the situation have all the personal sophistication necessary to enable them to appreciate the importance of the institutional setting in which their research occurs. Even if the investigator is personally insensitive, his informant may sooner or later draw the investigator's attention to institutional changes. This is, in fact, one of the advantages of the less structured research methods (unstructured interviewing and observation), when they are employed in this field. They allow a freedom of response to the informant and hence a degree of enlightenment to the investigator, which may not be as easily obtained through more structured methods. Their successful use in the Bank Wiring Observation Room influenced profoundly the methodology of later studies in this field. Because of the increased use of question-naires, unstructured interviewing and observation are now employed relatively less frequently than they were at one time. Yet their utility is such—particularly in the exploratory phases of industrial research, when there is a premium on suggestive ideas—that they are most unlikely to be abandoned altogether.

A powerful and somewhat surprising plea in favor of this comprehensive but distinctly psychologically oriented kind of study was recently made by Herbert Blumer in his presidential address to the American Sociological Society.[18] While Blumer looks forward to the ultimate existence of a systematic body of knowledge about the process of interpretation (a "scheme of sociological analysis" to handle the "diversified process of definition"[19]), he realizes that in the preliminary "effort to ferret out lines of definition," we shall have to rely on "a distinctive form of procedure" of an apparently rather clinical, nonsystematic kind. Blumer states that this procedure consists of an approach to "the study of group activity through the eyes and experience of the people who have developed the activity. Hence, it necessarily requires an intimate familiarity with this experience and with the scene of its operation. It uses broad and interlacing observations and not narrow and disjunctive observations."[20] Such weighting toward the psychological and toward the use of unstructured methods, therefore, which characterizes *Management and the Worker* could well be defended by the above quotation, as could some of the book's hasty shifts from one subject-matter area to another along with its lack of methodological polish.

It can thus be argued that there is a class of studies which is characteristically eclectic, comprehensive and somewhat psychologically oriented; that *Management and the Worker* belongs to this class; and that the class has a potential for making a substantial contribution to a field of inquiry, par-

[18]*"Sociological Analysis and the 'Variable',"* Presidential address read at the annual meeting of the American Sociological Society, September 1956, and reprinted in *American Sociological Review*, Vol. 21, No. 6, 1956, pp. 683–689.
[19]*Ibid.*, p. 689.   [20]*Ibid.*

ticularly when that field is a relatively unexplored one. We shall now document this latter point for the Hawthorne Studies by showing that they could be used to advantage for certain specific corrective purposes, and that they actually have been used and might have been used still further as a stimulant to sociological and social psychological studies of industrial problems.

The Corrective Function of a Comprehensive Study: Two Examples from MANAGEMENT AND THE WORKER

Class Consciousness and the Hawthorne Studies. One of the areas of specialized investigation to which the book and others of its kind could well bring enlightenment is that of the impact of occupational diversification on class consciousness and conflict. It may seem unnecessarily daring to praise the book for contributing to an area of which most critics have said that a case study of a single plant can add nothing. Friedmann[21] is one of those who regard class consciousness as an emergent phenomenon, understandable only when the investigator realizes that the experiences of workers in one factory are similar to those of his neighbors working in other factories. Only as a result of such shared experiences do classes grow and become of importance. But to agree that the shared character of work experiences plays an indispensable role in the formation of class consciousness need not, and should not, prevent one from looking upon the role of these experiences itself as equally indispensable. Both are necessary; neither is sufficient.

Management and the Worker presents a very sensitive picture of the forces which today draw classes together and pull them apart. Differences in levels of income; the worker's economic and status insecurity; his subordination in a large impersonal organization; differences in past background and in present interests; new barriers to social mobility in the form of educational requirements for promotion—they all

[21]"Philosophy Underlying the Hawthorne Investigations," *Social Forces*, Vol. 28, 1949, pp. 204–209.

tend to produce a clearer differentiation between workers and management, and they are all described to greater or lesser extent in *Management and the Worker*. Even the accession to working-class strength which Marx predicted under the heading of "the proletarization of the lower middle classes," can be illustrated within the Hawthorne Studies from the manner in which lower supervisors are described as identifying more with the operatives than with management, and their consequent failure to support management.

At the same time, however, the authors also portray the forces tending to reduce interclass hostility, and they supply the reader with data describing the manner in which interclass conflict is obscured because each side is splintered into subgroups. The split between white-collar and blue-collar workers is the most outstanding example of this, and the authors recognize this as basic enough to include it in their description of the plant as a social system composed of five groups (the other three groups being managers, engineers and supervisors). Other divisive forces of which there is evidence are ethnic friction among workers, a division between the sexes, the aloofness of highly trained workers possessing skills easily marketable outside the plant, the aloofness of groups of workers with middle-class aspirations, and the generally confused but also volatile state of mind of young workers caught in the process of changing cultures. *Management and the Worker* and descriptive studies like it are capable of presenting the reader with a very accurate snapshot of what the state of the nation is at any given point in time with respect to such elusive conditions as class consciousness. They can give him a fairly good picture, and one not obtainable in other ways, of what forces are at work producing just that particular state. In works where these forces are treated separately, the reader will find that each one is described more clearly: for example, the class struggle is more thoroughly analyzed by Marx, he will find the technocrats' ascendance portrayed more explicitly by Burnham,[22] and he will find the divisive forces within

[22] James Burnham, *The Managerial Revolution* (New York: John Day Company, 1934).

all groups described in more detail by Mills[23] and Moore.[24] But by definition, he can find all these approaches placed in their natural setting only in the type of study which seeks to do just that. And as an example of that type of study, *Management and the Worker* with all its shortcomings will retain a place.

The Nature and Place of "Economic" Variables. In order to illustrate the value of a comprehensive study in putting a specialist approach into perspective, one need not even go beyond *Management and the Worker.* For the book itself, while it covers much more ground than a modern rigorous study, does of course emphasize some areas of theoretical interest more than others. Of this we have already taken cognizance through a quotation (see p. 59 above) in which the authors indicated that they would confine their attention to "some neglected aspects" of the relationship between the worker and his job, for example, his social status in the company for which he works. Although the authors give no sign whatever of appreciating it, they themselves provide the reader with data which would tend to "cut down to size" (to use Dunlop's phrase) the importance in their productivity studies of precisely those aspects in which they were particularly interested. For while there was every reason to praise the authors for having been sufficiently comprehensive in their interests at least to note that the depression profoundly interfered with the progress of their studies in the Mica Splitting Test Room (p. 153), they give no indication that they drew any kind of basic theoretical conclusions from this interference. What seems to have occurred in the Mica Splitting Test Room, however, was that the authors' experimental variable was completely overwhelmed by another in which they had no interest. In the same vein the authors' failure to comment on the fact that the operators in the Bank Wiring Observation Room were put on progressively shorter hours

[23]C. Wright Mills, *White Collar* (New York: Oxford University Press, 1953).
[24]Wilbert E. Moore, "Occupational Structure and Conflict," in Kornhauser *et. al.,* eds., *Industrial Conflict* (New York: McGraw-Hill Book Co., Inc., 1954).

is even more startling, particularly since the authors' main thesis would still have stood the test of scrutiny. For the Bank wiremen's output was roughly the same during the observation period as during the base period (when hours were normal), reinforcing the authors' view that output control is but a part of a complex web of stable group relationships—it is not an individual's adaptation to a specific situation, economic or otherwise.

Whatever the authors' personal deficiency in interpretation, however, the mere presentation of data which allows others to judge the contribution of any discipline or variable, illustrates the merits of the comprehensive approach. Nor should it be lightly concluded, as in the case of resistance to change, that the authors in describing the Mica Splitting Test Room had once again merely demonstrated the obvious—this time unwittingly. For it should be remembered that no study or body of theory up to that time had included within its purview the effect of expected unemployment on attitudes toward productivity. While "growing unemployment" may be an economic variable from one point of view, it becomes operative and its effects on productivity become understandable only via a series of social and psychological mechanisms which no economist normally tackles.

We shall not speculate elsewhere on the reasons both for the authors' failure to do more than note briefly the psychological impact of economic factors which we have just noted, and for the authors' even more astonishing halt at the factory gates of the Hawthorne plant, before including its environment within their theoretical schema. However, some interpretation of the authors' personal stand must be included in this monograph if it is to be complete. Without going into detail, therefore, let it be said here that we agree with the critics that these omissions were not accidental, and that they represent, in all probability, a not unusual, but still highly regrettable, timidity in drawing basic conclusions which might have proven unpopular with the "powers-that-be." Such reluctance may well have been reinforced by the fact that those in power up to the very last had been friendly and helpful to the research and to the investigators themselves. A further reason for these omissions is probably that, like most innovators in the realm of ideas, the authors take up a position that is much more extreme and crude than are later versions of it. Moreover, at the time of the book's publication, it was not altogether a strategic error to emphasize, or rather to overemphasize the "social" as against the "economic" man of nineteenth century economic theory, and as against the "mechanical" and "physiological" man of industrial psychology.

The Stimulating Function of a Comprehensive Study: The Development of Human Relations—A Cautionary Tale

We have so far emphasized only one use—that of putting the influence of specific and already known variables into context—to which *Management and the Worker* can be put because of its comprehensive nature. In the case of human relations in industry, however, a far more important use of a book such as this was that of stimulating attention to the field as a whole by showing that fruitful, empirical research was possible. This function of the comprehensive study is particularly important when a potential field of inquiry has not previously been the object of attention from the various theoretical disciplines relevant to it. In the case of *Management and the Worker,* this point is obvious enough for authors like Whyte who maintained the tradition of empirical social investigation in industry in the years immediately following the publication of the Hawthorne Studies. These writers have acknowledged their debt to Harvard and have not explicitly sought to dissociate themselves from its theoretical position as they have interpreted it.

The debt may well be equally as large, however, in the case of authors who quite specifically reject some or all of the assumptions of the Mayo group. Even if, as Blumer thinks, the Harvard approach overemphasized the static and traditional qualities of labor-management relationships, it is presumably easier to formulate the right approach (in terms of power struggles between organizations in an everchanging environment) once some mistakes have been clearly made. The wrong approach *may* at least spell out the relevant dimensions (for example, static—dynamic) even if it ends up at the wrong end of each dimension! Whether later writers have sought to substantiate the findings of the book, have sought to disprove them, or have attempted to demonstrate yawning gaps in the work, there can be little doubt of the tremendous impetus which the Hawthorne Studies gave to sociological and social psychological studies of industrial problems. In fact, for at least ten years after the publication of *Management and the Worker,* the history of the field of human relations in industry was an explicit elaboration of one of the book's basic points, namely, that morale is related to supervision. The distortion of emphasis in which such one-sided elaboration resulted began to be corrected in the early 1950's. By this time, however, the Hawthorne Studies had become identified, both in the critics' mind and in the mind of students in the field, with the single point on which attention had been focused. The extent to which data—sometimes substantial, sometimes merely embryonic—for today's much broader research can be found in the pioneer study tends, therefore, to be forgotten. We shall draw attention to it in the following paragraphs.

Research on the Psychology of Supervision—the Original Impact. The stimulating effect of the Hawthorne Studies was most immediately and most powerfully felt in the area of first level supervision. Lewin's concurrent interest in autocratic and democratic styles of leadership also had its effect here, but the large amount of effort that has gone into research on, exhortation about, and training in supervision in industry in the last twenty years can probably be attributed more to the Hawthorne Studies than to any other single influence emanating from the academic world. In fact, it seemed to some critics in the late 1940's that human relations in industry as a field of study was coterminous with this much narrower aspect of it. Whyte's *Human Relations in the Restaurant Industry,* based on studies inspired by the Hawthorne experiments, treats supervisory problems at great length, and has been criticized for this.[25] The Michigan studies, about different kinds of supervisor-worker relationships, were also inspired in part by the Hawthorne Studies but followed a more rigorous, if less rich path than did Whyte's qualitative work. Yet another group of studies, dealing with the inherent difficulties of the supervisor's position on the margins of management,[26] also appeared at this time and can likewise be traced back to data from the Hawthorne Studies.[27] Apart from empirical research, there accrued at this time a plethora of books, test manuals, and pamphlets, all dealing essentially with "how to be an effective supervisor." Most of these writings, as well as the research previously cited, were explicitly or implicitly based on two assumptions, the truth of which was supposedly demonstrated by the Hawthorne Studies— although we have already seen that this was far from being the case. The first of these assumptions was that the state of the supervisor-worker relationship is determined by the supervisor's personal skill. The second assumption is that these skill-determined supervisor-worker relationships in turn determine important phenomena such as job satisfaction and productivity, and even possibly satisfaction or discontent with the company as a whole and with the industrial system generally.

Since the face-to-face explanation of worker-management conflict had little place in *Management and the Worker,* and was—as we have already shown in Chapter IV above, in the section, *Anomie and the Causes of Industrial Conflict*—at one point explicitly eschewed by it's authors, it is of interest to

[25]Willam F. Whyte, *Human Relations in the Restaurant Industry* (New York: McGraw-Hill Book Co., Inc., 1948). Like the Hawthorne Studies, this book contains so much other rich material (concerning, for example, the effect of technology on interpersonal relations, and the relation between social background and attitudes) that the criticism is hardly just.

[26]See, for example, Donald E. Wray, "Marginal Men of Industry: The Foreman," *American Journal of Sociology,* Vol. 54, 1949, p. 293–301.

[27]*Management and the Worker,* pp. 448, et seq.

speculate briefly why the book should have been so dramatically misinterpreted both by its enemies and by its friends. Why was this point singled out for attention to the exclusion of all but one other point (reactions to incentive systems) raised in the book?

The critics' imbalanced assessment of the book probably resulted from the fact that they failed to retain the distinction between it and later studies written by persons known to be associated with the Mayo school who subsequently made points which were quite different from those made in the original study. This failure was in turn probably caused by the critics' failure to give the book itself the independent scrutiny which it deserves. In any case, Scott and Homans' "Reflections on the Wildcat Strikes,"[28] and Mayo and Lombard's treatment of labor turnover[29], did indeed emphasize the personal skill of the supervisor as a determinant of various industrial phenomena. These studies have added a great deal of grist to the critics' mill, since few critics are aware that they have little in common with *Management and the Worker*.

It may be noted here, too, that the critics are in danger of going to the equally erroneous opposite extreme of asserting that supervision, and the skill with which it is carried out, has no influence whatever on the worker's attitude to his job. This in its turn would be a dubious position to take in the light of the Michigan studies.[30] Those with practical experience in industry feel certain that the quality of supervision has improved immeasurably in the last twenty years, that this has not been without effect on the work force, and that training (temporary research evidence notwithstanding![31]) and the Hawthorne Studies have had much to do with the improvement.

[28]Jerome C. Scott and George C. Homans, "Reflections on the Wildcat Strikes," *American Sociological Review*, Vol. 11, 1947, pp. 278–287.

[29]Elton Mayo and George F. Lombard, *Teamwork and Labor Turnover in the Aircraft Industry of Southern California* (Cambridge: Harvard University Graduate School of Business Administration, 1944).

[30]Cf. Nancy Morse, *op. cit.*

[31]See Edwin F. Harris and Edwin Fleischman, "Human Relations and the Stability of Leadership Patterns," *Journal of Applied Psychology*, Vol. 39, No. 1, 1955, pp. 20–25.

Misinterpretation of the Hawthorne Studies by its friends in and out of academic life is less easy to explain. In part, there has not really been a misinterpretation, but simply a concentration by later researchers on only one of the many problems raised by the original studies (and the personal skill of supervisors did, of course, figure in the studies to some extent). Such temporary concentration need not involve any gross exaggeration of the importance of the variable which one has selected for investigation, since selection is a prerequisite for rigorous study no matter what one's belief. Critics have often failed to make this distinction.

Nevertheless, it is probably true that those academicians who have followed the course which they saw the Hawthorne Studies as setting, and certainly those in industry who have used the studies, have been guilty of some distortion, and for this the explanation lies once again in the emotional times during which the book was published. For if some sociologists were at that time concerned about finding a theory which would explain the violent movements of the late thirties, others were less oriented toward explanation and were more concerned with finding methods which would enable one to deal with these disturbances. The motive for such concern need not be—as is sometimes imputed—that of pleasing property owners or busting unions, although some individuals will undoubtedly be so motivated. It may simply flow from a very sincere dislike of social strife and discontent and a conviction that it is harmful. This position is as old as any in social philosophy, with as many good arguments on its side as on the side of those who emphasize the positive social functions of conflict. But whatever the ultimate motive behind the concern about social discontent, that concern is more easily allayed if the analysis of the causes of discontent is portrayed as simple and the remedies prescribed for them as easy to administer. Given the turmoil of the forties, it was reassuring to locate its causes at the shop-floor level, and cherish at least temporarily the illusion that these causes were circumscribed, diagnosed, and controllable. It postponed the evil day on which the

104

ramified nature of these causes would have to be recognized, and the time when it would be necessary to trace them into the higher reaches of management and beyond that, into the economic and social environment.

But the nature of facts is such that they will not let themselves be obscured permanently. Hence the history of the field of human relations since the late forties has been a slow and painful discovery of the myriad of complex factors which really do determine the quality of human relationships in industry. And as the field has broadened, it has become progressively more closely linked to traditional areas of theory and investigation in the already established social sciences.

The Study of Bureaucracy. The study of supervision merged into a study of industrial bureaucracy as a whole, once it was recognized that: (a) analytically speaking, problems of supervision could arise at any level in the hierarchy and were equivalent to problems of authority with which bureaucratic theory has long concerned itself; and (b) the foreman's style of supervising others depended not only on his personality, but also on the supervision he received from his superiors.[32] This resulted, in the first instance, in directing attention toward the top of the industrial hierarchy. On the research side, it resulted in books such as Argyris' *Executive Leadership;*[33] on the training side, it has resulted in efforts such as those reported in the later Michigan studies.[34]

Of late, however, there has been a growing recognition that industrial bureaucracy, or organization, may contain inherent rigidities which make the outlook for any kind of training bleaker than had originally been thought, since organization is now viewed, by its very nature, as tending to constrict the individuals within it.[35] The evolution of Argyris' views epi-

[32]Daniel Katz, Nathan Maccoby, Nancy Morse, *Productivity, Supervision and Morale in an Office Situation* (Ann Arbor: University of Michigan, 1951), Part I, p. 36.

[33]Chris Argyris, *Executive Leadership* (New York: Harper & Brothers, 1950).

[34]As reported in, for example, *Training in Human Relations,* and also in *Planning and Training for Effective Leadership,* both published by the Foundation for Research on Human Behavior, Ann Arbor, Michigan, 1954–1955.

[35]Argyris, *Personality and the Organization: The Conflict Between System and the Individual* (New York: Harper & Brothers, 1957).

tomizes this dramatic change in the field of human relations. He had originally been among the most vigorous in advocating the efficacy of first level supervisory training,[36] shifting later toward greater emphasis on psychological skills at the senior management level.[37] His present concern with personal dissatisfactions which are endemic to organization, and partly independent of the personality of those manning it at any level, brings research back to the stage where the Hawthorne Studies, correctly interpreted, might well have left it some twenty years ago. The shift in interest from first level supervision to the industrial authority structure as a whole certainly links research to traditional writings in sociology, such as those of Max Weber[38] and Robert Merton.[39]

Indeed, the Hawthorne Studies are replete with contributions to the study of bureaucracy, and data may be found there which shed light on problems not explicitly formulated till several years later. Reisman,[40] for example, has noted that professionals—such as engineers, lawyers, architects—may adopt one of several solutions to the problem of whether they should primarily identify with the organization which hired them as specialists, or with the profession of which they are members, thus remaining psychologically rather aloof from the organization in which they are actually working. Yet in nascent form, the peculiar relationship between the organization and the specialist with outside training was already described by Roethlisberger and Dickson when they discovered that those supervisors who had served an apprenticeship and had worked in companies other than Western Electric "seemed to have a feeling of security that did not depend on their relationship to the company alone. Their feelings had

[36]*Role Playing in Action* (Ithaca: New York State School of Industrial and Labor Relations at Cornell University, Bulletin No. 16, 1951).

[37]*Executive Leadership, op. cit.*

[38]*From Max Weber: Essays in Sociology,* trans. and ed. by H. H. Gerth and C. Wright Mills (New York: Oxford University Press, 1946), pp. 196–244.

[39]Robert K. Merton, "Bureaucratic Structure and Personality," *Social Forces,* Vol. 18, 1940, pp. 560–568.

[40]Leonard Reisman, "A Study of Role Conceptions in Bureaucracy," *Social Forces,* Vol. 27, 1949, pp. 305–310.

a maturity which seemed to be lacking in some other supervisors" (p. 353).

The whole problem, too, of the foreman as the man in the middle (first raised in *Management and the Worker*) is of course common to all hierarchies. No matter whether one is dealing with the army, the factory, the hospital or the union, the problem will arise whether the first level supervisor should be oriented and identified with his superior or his subordinates. One may cite, too, the authors' early analysis of informal relationships as aids and obstacles to reaching organizational goals;[41] and finally one may mention their analysis of the frictions which arise between functionally separate groups in organizations, such as technicians and line personnel, or between shop and office workers.

In part, problems of this kind may be viewed as merely an aspect of a power struggle between social classes in society at large. But there is much reason to think that these problems are by no means confined to capitalist societies and therefore comprehensible only in their context. On the contrary, these problems are likely to be found in any type of organization simply because it is an organization, and within wide limits regardless of the type of society in which the organization is found.[42]

Developments in Human Relations in Industry— Their Roots and Direction

Not only bureaucracy, but other areas of interest to sociologists are being explored now that the narrow optimism and psychological overemphasis of the supervisory studies are being overcome. Many of these newer areas were already embedded in the Hawthorne Studies and even in the writings of the much maligned Mayo himself. The community inte-

[41]This point is further explored particularly by Melville Dalton. See his article, "Managing the Managers," *Human Organization*, Vol. 14, 1955, pp. 4–10.

[42]For a recent exposition of this view, see George C. Homans, "Industrial Harmony as a Goal," in Kornhauser *et al., op. cit.,* pp. 48–58. Homans' view is anything but optimistic, and while he defends—as the title implies— harmony as a goal, he describes and promises no simple remedies of any kind.

gration-disintegration variable, for example, and its relation
to industrial strife has recently been given a prominent place
by two authors who had been among the severest critics of the
Mayo school. Kerr and Siegel,[43] discussing interindustry differences in the propensity to strike, argue that individuals
isolated from the community as a whole but themselves form-
ing a tight community (such as miners) will have a high propensity to strike, whereas individuals not attached to their
fellow workers but well integrated into the general community (such as office workers) will not engage in overt
organized conflict. Mayo focused on the same two variables,
the individual's integration into the work group and his integration into the community, and parts of the Hawthorne
Studies also deal with these questions. Both Mayo and the
authors of the Hawthorne Studies discuss one of the two
remaining logical alternatives: individuals who were isolated
both from the general community *and* from their immediate
neighborhood. For them, participation in unorganized conflict (through, for example, absenteeism and restriction of output)[44] was predicted.[45]

The Interest-Group Approach. Long familiar to political
scientists and to sociologists interested in community structure and political processes, the interest-group approach is
another approach to which increasing attention has recently
had to be paid in the analysis of social data from industry. It
has, of course, always been a much favored approach to the
understanding of union-management relations. Not only have
critics of the human relations school employed it,[46] but even

[43]Clark Kerr and Abraham Siegel, "The Interindustry Propensity to Strike
—an International Comparison," pp. 188–212, in Kornhauser, *et al., op. cit.*

[44]For an approach equating absenteesism with other forms of conflict,
see Kornhauser *et al., op. cit.,* p. 16.

[45]Other students of the relation between industry and community values
and integration include, of course, Alvin Gouldner, whose books cover a wide
range of topics including this one and industrial bureaucracy. See his *Patterns
of Industrial Bureaucracy* (Glencoe, Ill.: Free Press, 1954), and *The Wildcat
Strike* (Yellow Springs, Ohio: Antioch Press, 1954).

[46]See, for example, Herbert Blumer, "Social Structure and Power Conflict,"
pp. 232–244 in Kornhauser *et al, op. cit.,* and Frederick Harbison and Robert
Dubin, *Patterns of Union Management Relations* (Chicago: Science Research
Associates, 1947).

writers like Whyte, who emphasizes primarily the importance
of face-to-face interactions, have never ruled out analysis in
terms of conflicts of interest. Unfortunately, statements that
"the functions of a local union...may be roughly divided into
two categories: *protective* and *integrative*. As protective, we
think of those functions which...involve a recognition of different interests and are essentially efforts to maintain or
improve the position of the union as compared to management"[47] are never quoted by Whyte's critics, while statements
in which he extols the virtues and possibilities of union-management cooperation are invariably quoted.

The conflict-of-interest paradigm is such a good one, however, that its applicability extends far beyond organized,
union-management relations. Sayles and Strauss already
utilized it extensively to explain internal union affairs at the
local level,[48] thus following and elaborating upon the work of
institutional economists like Ross who had applied the
approach to union wage policy formulation.[49] The only area
to which the interest-group approach has not been applied is
that of internal management structure, and the author and
a colleague are currently doing just that.[50]

It cannot be claimed that *Management and the Worker* did,
in fact, inspire later researchers to utilize this approach in the
same way as, for example, it directly inspired research into
small-group leadership. What can legitimately be said, however, is that the book's failure to provide such inspiration
was less its fault than that of its readers. The data on the
formation of groups presented by the authors, and their
analysis of that data in Chapter XXIII, invited an interest-
group explanation as much as any other (as we were at pains
to point out in the previous chapter). The authors' presenta-

[47]William F. Whyte, *Pattern for Industrial Peace* (New York: Harper &
Brothers, 1951), p. 217.

[48]*Op. cit.*, particularly chapters 5, 6, 7, and 11.

[49]Arthur M. Ross, *Trade Union Wage Policy* (Berkeley: University of California Press, 1948).

[50]Henry A. Landsberger and Frank B. Miller, "An Addition to Bureaucratic
Theory: Conceptualizing the Neglected Horizontal Dimension," paper read at
the annual meeting of the American Sociological Society, September 1957
(mimeo.).

tion is analytically less clear-cut than if they had sought to establish this approach above all others. Yet their unpointed description of how the interests of one group may be harmed by the actions of another in pursuit of its interests, gains in retrospect just because it enables us to see how much a clash of interests is often obscured by other, more obvious aspects of the situation (such as overt dislike of an unpopular supervisor).

It should be noted that a conflict-of-interest analysis tends to lead the researcher toward a further area of investigation, that of the changing problems which each of the contending groups faces in its relations to its environment. In the case of the Hawthorne Studies, the worsened economic environment in which the Western Electric Company had to operate from 1930 onwards was described in several parts of the book, and was shown to affect not only the company's treatment of employees (toward whom much paternalistic benevolence had been shown up till then), but also of the researchers with whom the company had previously cooperated without reservation. That relationships between various groups in industry (even within management or within unions alone) can change, subsequent to changes in their environment, was thus at the very least hinted at by *Management and the Worker*. Since then, however, this area of investigation has been little pursued by sociologists, even by sociologists hostile to a purely in-plant approach. Yet it could be one of the most instructive lines of research, because the survival of each group in its environment is a prerequisite to all its other relationships and must therefore have a profound effect on them.

Technology and Human Relations. A further area of investigation, more reminiscent of the growth of human relations studies out of industrial psychology than of their link to sociology, is that of the relationship between technology and human relations. This area includes, of course, tracing the effects of technological factors on supervision and on the structure of small working groups, as well as on the relationship between workers and management as a whole.[51] On this topic too, *Management and the Worker* contains pertinent data. Witness, for example, the difference between social relationships in the various test rooms where no one was dependent on anyone else by virtue of his job, and the complex, ambivalent relationships in the Bank Wiring Observation Room where, partly through the nature of the job, some workers were subordinate to others in the matter of skill while controlling them so far as work-flow was concerned. Possible effects a worker's location might have on his social status and relationships were also recognized (p. 496).

The work of Walker and his associates at Yale[52] has recently dealt most fully with the psychological and interpersonal characteristics of the job itself, while writers such as Chinoy,[53] starting with the same problem area, have concentrated more on tracing its social implications. Both these writers have returned to the investigation of one of the traditional areas of industrial psychology—that of monotony. But they have brought to it a sensitiveness to the sociological and psychological effects of monotony which had previously been lacking.

The Place of Financial Reward. There is a further area of research which *Management and the Worker* so patently opened up, that not even the subsequent preoccupation with supervision could submerge it completely. Under continual investigation since the early forties, the place of financial reward did not have to be rediscovered some ten years later. We refer particularly to investigations of the determinants of workers' reactions to various systems of payment. The most recent and comprehensive treatment of this topic is to be

[51]For early hints that the optimal type of supervision varies with the kind of job being supervised, see Daniel Katz, Nathan Maccoby, Gerald Gurin, Lucretia G. Floor, *Productivity, Supervision and Morale Among Railroad Workers* (Ann Arbor: University of Michigan, 1952), p. 33.

[52]See, for example, Charles Walker and Robert H. Guest, *The Man on the Assembly Line* (Cambridge: Harvard University Press, 1952). The tone of this book is notably somber and like most latter-day writings on in-plant matters shows no signs of the easy optimism of the past decade.

[53]Ely Chinoy, *Automobile Workers and the American Dream* (Garden City, N. Y.: Doubleday & Co., 1955).

found in Whyte's *Money and Motivation*.[54] But several of the studies reported there go back ten years or more. These earlier studies were intended as further investigations of the restriction-of-output phenomenon revealed by the Hawthorne Studies: why, and under what circumstances, workers would restrict output rather than take advantage of an incentive system to maximize current monetary income. Roethlisberger and Dickson's discovery that such restriction did take place, and that it was linked, *inter alia,* to the structure of the small face-to-face groups in which workers worked, was, to the academic world, at least as startling as were their findings on supervision. Since this discovery, the phenomena (and reactions to monetary incentives in general) have been related not only to small group structure, but to the values of different ethnic groups,[55] to organizational variables,[56] and to the nature of the job and the satisfaction to be obtained from it.

Special Groups and Special Needs. Finally, there remains one area which has not been investigated to any great extent, but on which the Hawthorne Studies have again already shed some light. We drew attention early in this monograph to the fact that some of the behavior described by the authors may well have been characteristic of the age, cultural, and socioeconomic level from which the workers whom they observed were drawn. Older, skilled workers might well have reacted differently to the Bank Wiring Observation Room than did the fairly young semiskilled group whom the authors observed. This is likely to be so because, certainly, different individuals have different needs and values, and will therefore react differently to the same situation. But while such differences are indeed ultimately individual, comparisons of averages across certain groups will not prove useless, since groups do, to some extent, have similar needs. Thus a male

[54]Willam F. Whyte, *Money and Motivation* (New York: Harper & Brothers, 1955).

[55]Melville Dalton, "Worker Response to Wage Incentives in Relation to Social Background," *Journal of Political Economy,* Vol. 55, 1947, pp. 323–332.

[56]Donald Roy, "Efficiency and the Fix," *American Journal of Sociology,* Vol. 60, No. 3, (Nov. 1954), pp. 230–245.

worker in his twenties will, on the whole, be more interested than a married woman worker in the chances for advancement associated with the job at which each is working. Such differences in what is looked for from work probably have a profound influence on what types of work situations are considered satisfying. The sociologists and social psychologists of industry have tended to neglect what could be one of the most fruitful areas of research chiefly because they have been more interested in exploring social relations and entire organizational structures than in comparing individuals and groups. Once again, however, a careful rereading of *Management and the Worker* reveals an area of research which was potentially opened up by the authors.

Summary and Conclusion

This monograph has had two purposes. First, we have attempted to show that many of the criticisms which have been leveled against Mayo do not apply to *Management and the Worker*. We reviewed briefly the contents of *Management and the Worker*, showing how through a series of admitted trials and errors, the authors finally defined the core of their research problem as being that of exploring what, in the work situation, determined the attitudes of those within it. Our review established that the authors could not be accused of (1) being biased in management's favor; (2) that they did not regard workers as being spurred on by irrational motives; (3) that they did not regard the factory as a suitable replacement for a vanished primitive society; and (4) that they did not regard the formation of groups as being caused by any instinct, but rather saw it as a reaction of workers to threats by management. This brought us to the authors' description of the conflict situation at Hawthorne. Startling as it may seem, a case can be made for stating that Roethlisberger and Dickson described the conflict at Hawthorne in terms which are quite congruent with the type of analysis which an economic determinist would have made in the same situation. However, the authors did not pursue their analysis so far as to consider factors such as property ownership, size of organization, and general technological change. Instead, they concluded their book with a rather unconvincing description of the counseling program which they propose as a method for reducing the tensions they have described.

At this point, our re-evaluation broadened into a more general discussion of the type of study which *Management and the Worker* is and must be looked upon as being a representative. It was noted that the book was in essence a descriptive study presenting data of relevance to a variety of disciplines and subdisciplines; that such a study can be expected to be of the greatest value when a certain social problem area—human relations in industry—has not been investigated before; and in particular, that such a study may be expected to serve the functions of putting specialist approaches into their place and—at the same time—of stimulating further inquiries by various specialists. We noted that *Management and the Worker,* while covering many topics, did at the same time focus more on (a) the effect of the situation on individual attitudes, and (b) the effect of attitudes on subsequent individual behavior rather than on the structure of the situation itself. It was maintained that this focus on the individual's definition of, and reaction to, the situation in which he finds himself is indispensable to a complete understanding of social action in general and social conflict in particular. The intensive, complete study of a few situations and of the individuals within them, by means of unstructured interviewing and observation, was likely to yield much rich data on what precisely "the situation" really was. In addition, such study is essential to a prediction of how the individual would react to the situation.

The dangers of relying too heavily on the perceptions and behavior of a limited number of individuals must, at the same time, be cited. These dangers lie, as the critics have pointed out, in paying insufficient attention to institutional developments, although we noted that some representatives of the human relations school have paid a great deal of attention to such developments, even if Roethlisberger and Dickson failed to do so. However, even at the level at which human relations researchers are most expert, namely that of the individual's definition of the situation, there is a danger that researcher and informant alike—if they concentrate on the informant's definition—will underestimate the importance of factors in the situation to which the informant is responding, but of which he can never be aware except by means of contrast with other situations in which he is not involved. Yet even in the explanation of strikes (where the limitations of the human relations approach with its focus on individuals and small groups have been most apparent), that approach may ultimately have rather more to contribute than seems likely at the moment. We have seen that even critics of the approach, such as Kerr and Siegel, have in fact had to rely on a theory which stresses the attitudes of the individual, and the individual's relationship to fellow workers and to the community at large.

Far outweighing its limitations is the positive effect which *Management and the Worker* had (1) in showing that empirical research within industry and organizations in general was at all possible; (2) in broadening and profoundly changing one well-established subdiscipline, that of industrial psychology; and (3) in touching upon most of the problem areas into which the field of human relations in industry is now breaking up. This breakup was delayed for some ten years by a misreading of the lessons of the book not only by its critics, but also by its friends. Now that the error can no longer be overlooked, the field of human relations is becoming a more sober one, and its various subparts are forging links with branches and theories of the more established social sciences. But most of these later developments were, or could have been, foreshadowed by the Hawthorne Studies, and all have been stimulated by the courage shown by the authors of the book in conducting studies of this kind in the first place.

The authors of *Management and the Worker* need not hang their heads in shame, for the book is indeed a classic. We suggest that in the future more light will be shed on the entire field if, as a minimum concession, the attackers avoid shooting at innocent bystanders. Preferably, of course, the battle might now cease altogether—has not progress been such as to remove most of the legitimate targets?

Index

Anomie, 29–30, 44, 63–73; and community changes, 82, 107–8
Anthropology, 29, 30, 35, 36, 72, 83
Argyris, Chris, 3, 105–6
Aspirations and expectations of individuals, determinants of, 19, 21, 97, 113; effects of, 18
Attitudes, 15–21; determinants of, 20, 21–2, 101, 102, 113, 114; of employees to productivity, 24, 38, 49, 98–9; of supervisors, 54

Bank Wiring Observation Room, 22–7; analysis of, 59, 98–9, 112; atmosphere in, 58, 74, 111; observer in, 23; relationship between operators, 61–2, 66–8, 111; research methods in, 22, 94; supervision of, 75
Bell, Daniel, 28n, 33–4, 37, 40, 51n
Bendix, Reinhard, 28n, 31–2, 68n, 81n, 88
Blumer, Herbert, 28n, 32–3, 42, 44–5, 88, 95, 100, 108n
Bureaucracy, 44, 83, 89, 105–7

Catharsis, 30, 54, 75
Collaboration see Conflict
Collective bargaining, 39–43, 87; see also Conflict
Communications, 25, 30, 40–3, 68, 74
Community see Anomie
Competition see Conflict
Conflict, 28–47, 62, 63–73, 82, 96–8, 108–10, 113, 115
Cooperation see Conflict
Counseling, 27, 37, 40, 47, 54, 70, 75–9

Dunlop, John T., 28n, 41–2. 43, 68, 98

Economic circumstances of workers, 57–60
Economic environment, 2, 82–3; effect on management-worker relations, 20, 33, 42, 43, 69, 74, 110; effect on worker, 20, 57, 72

Economic security see Security of job
Elite, 31, 32, 33
Engineers, 23, 26, 62, 65, 69, 107

Fatigue see Productivity
Freeman, Ellis, 28n, 35–6
Friedmann, Georges, 28n, 78, 96

Gilson, Mary B., 1, 21, 45, 51
Groups see Work Groups

Hart, C. W. M., 28n, 34–5, 44, 52, 72n, 81n
Harvard group see Mayo school
Hawthorne Studies, 1, 2; explanatory theories in, 15, 20, 21, 23, 26–7, 59–60, 61, 64, 65, 86–100, 104; planning, 4; research methods employed in, 22, 23, 90, 114–15; summary of, 4–27; tentativeness of, 5, 15, 22, 25, 48–51; see also listing of individual experiments of Hawthorne Studies; see also Management and the Worker
Homans, George C., 2n, 62n, 68, 83n; and Jerome C. Scott, 103, 107n
Human relations, the field of, and manipulation, 21, 36–7; areas covered by, 2, 101–15; assessments of, 3, 69; criticisms of, 28–47; definition of, 81–5; development of, 80–115; methodology of, 83–5; question of validity, 2; training, 2; see also listing of individual studies of Hawthorne experiments; see also Mayo school

Illumination experiments, 5–7
Image of the worker, 30, 35–9, 55–63
Industrial psychology, 86–8, 90, 111
Industrial sociology see Sociology
Informal groups and leaders see Work Groups
Interviewing program and method, anal-

ysis of comments, 17, 19, 20, 53–4; and human relations, 83; and manipulation, 36; and sociological theory, 94–6; counseling, 27; development of, 16, 17, 19, 23, 54; *see also* Counseling program

Institutions *see* Social class and social structure

Irrationality *see* Image of the worker

Katz, Daniel, Nathan Maccoby, and Nancy Morse, 55n, 84n, 105n; and Nathan Maccoby, Gerald Gurin, and Lucretia G. Floor, 111n

Kerr, Clark, 28n, 30–1, 48, 72n, 73; and Lloyd Fisher, 82n; 108, 115

Koivisto, W. A., 29n, 36, 38, 41

Kornhauser, Arthur, Robert Dubin, and Arthur M. Ross, 64n, 107n, 108n

Lewin, Kurt, 85, 101

Management, and sentiments, 79; and supervision, 25; and unions, 63–4; and utility of Hawthorne Studies, 15, 27, 59, 73–6; and workers, 32, 33, 35–9, 54, 62, 65–7, 70, 75, 96–7, 106, 111; effect of interest on employees, 16; expectations of workers, 23, 24; functions of, 74; reorganization by, 44; *see also* Economic environment

Management and the Worker, 2; and Elton Mayo, 3, 46–7; and Mayo school, 46–7; and sociological theory and method, 90–6; and timing, 4, 52, 88–9, 104; and unions, 51–6; criticisms of, 3, 48–79, 90–1, 93, 98, 103, 113, 114–15; evaluation of criticisms of, 48–79; *see also* Hawthorne Studies

Manipulation of employees, and counseling, 77–8; and Hawthorne Studies, 73, 78, 84–5; and supervisor training, 16, 21; by management, 56; by Mayo group, 35–9, 104

Marx, Karl, 71, 93, 94, 97

Mayo, Elton, and analysis of the Hawthorne Studies, 27; and anomie, 70–2, 108; and conflict, 31, 32, 68; and human relations in industry, 28; and informal groups, 61; and the Hawthorne experiments, 5; and the "rabble hypothesis," 86; and unions, 43–6; and view of workers, 35–9; approach compared with that in *Management and the Worker,* 3, 47–50, 61, 70–2; and George F. Lombard, 103; *see also* Mayo school

Mayo school, and image of workers, 30, 35–9, 55; and informal groups, 61; and management, 36–9; and research methodology, 35; and sociological theory, 35; and status strivings of workers, 30, 31, 57; and theory of conflict, 30–5, 63, 64; and theory of social change, 29–30; and unions, 30; criticisms of, 1, 2, 3, 28–47, 55, 61, 63, 81–5, 96, 100, 104, 108; development of, 2, 3, 80; *see also* Human relations; *see also* Manipulation

Mica Splitting Test Room, 13–15, 50; and effect of insecurity, 57, 98–9; compared with Relay Assembly Test Room, 13, 14, 61; compared with Second Relay Assembly Group, 13; productivity in, 14; relationship between operators, 61, 72

Michigan Studies, 84, 103, 105

Mills, C. Wright, 29n, 36–7, 38–9, 40–1, 45, 47n, 51, 98

Monotony *see* Productivity

Moore, Wilbert E., 29n, 35, 38, 44, 83, 84, 98

Morale *see* Attitudes

Norms *see* Work groups

Output, control of, *see* Productivity

Parsons, Talcott, 74

Personal preoccupations, and counseling program, 76–8; causes of, 20; of employees, 71–3; Mayo school's overemphasis on, 35, 37, 38, 40, 55, 92–6, 113–15; method of eliciting, 19

Personality, effect of industrial organization on, 35–6, 106

Productivity, and cooperation, 67–8; and determination by employee, 8; and fatigue, 11–12, 50, 88; and hours of work, 87; and illumination, 6–7, 86; and industrial conflict, 40; and length of working day, 7; and machine 'pacing', 8; and methods and materials, 11, 50; and monotony, 11–12, 50, 111; and rest pauses, 7–15, 86; and rivalry between groups, 13; and type of work, 6; and types of workers, 6; and wage incentives, 11, 12–15, 23, 69; control of, 23, 24, 25, 26, 65, 112; effect of declining employment, 14, 98–9; effect of employees' attitudes on, 16, 49, 75, 87–8; effect of isolating sub-groups, 9; effect of observer on, 23; effect of social relations on variability in, 14; measurement of, 8; *see also* listing of individual experiments of Hawthorne Studies; *see also* Supervision; *see also* Work groups

Psychiatric orientation of Hawthorne Studies *see* Personal preoccupations

Psychology *see* Personal preoccupations

Relay Assembly Test Room, 7, 8, 49–50; compared with Bank Wiring Observation Room, 67; compared with Mica Splitting Test Room, 14; compared with Second Relay Assembly Group, 13; consultation of operators in, 9–10, 15; function of observer in, 8, 10–11; productivity in, 10; records kept in, 8–9; relationship between operators in, 10, 61, 62, 67, 68, 72; strain to produce, 9; supervision of, 10, 15, 53, 75; system of payment in, 9, 12–13; *see also* Productivity; *see also* Management

Rest Pause experiments, 7–15, 16; *see also* listing of individual experiments in this series

Roethlisberger, F. J. and William J. Dickson, 2n, 4, 47, 50, 52, 57, 59, 63, 68, 79, 106, 112, 113, 115

Ross, Arthur, 64n, 109

Sayles, Leonard R. and George Strauss, 84n, 109

Schneider, E. V., 29n, 83

Schneider, Louis, 29n, 37, 39, 40

Second Relay Assembly Group, 12–13, 50; compared with Relay Assembly Test Room, 13, 75; productivity in, 12; system of payment in, 12

Security of job, and depression, 57–8, 98–9; and engineers, 65; and social class, 33, 96; effects on operators of, 15, 23, 50, 57–9, 62, 66

Selekman, Benjamin B., 51n, 52

Sentiments, 18, 19, 55–7, 74, 78–9, 94

Sheppard, Harold L., 29n, 32, 38, 40, 46

Siegel, Abraham J., 69n, 108, 115

Social class and social structure, 32, 33–4, 45, 46, 89, 93–4, 96–8, 107

Social mobility *see* Social class

Sociology, 35, 88–9, 90–3, 104–6, 110, 112

Sorenson, R. C., 29n, 34, 39–40, 68n

Special groups of workers, and social class, 96–7; ethnic groups and immigrants, 71, 89, 90, 112; men, 17, 59; office employees, 59, 65; shop workers, 59, 65; supervisors, 59, 65, 106–7; women, 17, 59, 71

Status, and industrial relations, 33, 40, 41; of different jobs, 59, 111; of supervisors, 20, 23, 25; of workers in factories, 26, 58–60, 61–2, 66, 82, 96

Supervision, ambiguous status of, 20, 23, 25, 65, 77, 97, 107; and counseling program, 76–7; and productivity, 15, 23; and technology, 110; and workers, 58, 62, 65; attitudes of, 54–5, 73, 106–7; in Relay Assembly Test Room, 10; styles of, 21, 66, 70, 75, 101–4; training for, 2, 16, 21, 66, 78, 105–6

Tead, Ordway, 29n, 45

Technological change, 27, 66, 69–70, 74–5, 114

Technologists *see* Engineers

Unions, 30, 31, 33, 41, 42, 43–7, 51–6, 58, 63–73, 84, 88, 104, 108–10

Veblen, Thorstein, 93

Wage incentives *see* Productivity

Wages, 56, 58, 59, 60, 62, 63, 65, 109, 111–12; *see also* Productivity, and individual experiments of the Hawthorne Studies

Warner, W. Lloyd, 82, 82n, 94

Western Electric Company, 4, 51, 52, 53, 55, 59

Whitehead, T. North, 1, 4, 11, 37, 46, 47

Whyte, William F., 2n, 83n, 100, 102, 109, 112

Work groups, and communication with management, 25; and control of output, 23, 24, 26, 65, 75, 112; and Mayo school, 30, 36; common environment and formation of, 21, 22; definition of, 21; factors affecting social relations in, 10, 14, 97–8, 110; informal leadership of, 23; measurement of social relations in, 26; norms of, 26; reaction of rest of department to, 13; reasons for rise of informal groups, 61–8, 79, 86, 113; relations with supervisors, 25, 84; social relations in, 25–6, 58, 60, 108